Bullying in Teams

How to Survive It and Thrive

Bullying in Teams

How to Survive It and Thrive

Aryanne Oade

Oade Associates trading as Flourish
c/o Oxford Literary Consultancy
Powerhouse Publications
Suite 124
94 London Road
Oxford OX3 9FN

www.oadeassociates.com
mail@oadeaassociates.com

978-0-9931391-4-7 Print
978-0-9931391-5-4 eBook

British Library Cataloguing in Publication Data

A catalogue record for his book is available from the British Library

Praise for *Bullying in Teams: How to Survive It and Thrive*

This book blows the lid off team bullying. Whether you've been the target of bullying, or a witness to it, this compassionate and insightful book reveals the tactics employed by team bullies and how to regain your emotional compass. It's a uniquely valuable tool for organisations and individuals alike and I wish I'd read it years ago.

Danai Pampiglione, HR Director

This is a powerful and insightful examination of the toxic impact of team bullying. Using real life examples, Aryanne Oade confronts the dynamics of power used by the bully and the impact on the wellbeing of the target and the team more broadly. The book is full of practical tools, techniques and tactics to help the reader understand how to change the power dynamics at the moment of attack. The positive message to take away is that resilience, and the use of effective self-protective and self-preserving behaviours, are learned skills, and that it is possible both to withstand the bullying and regain self-confidence and self-belief during or after a campaign.

Professor Norma Martin Clement, Pro-Dean, Faculty of Education Social Sciences and Law, University of Leeds

Culture by definition is the behaviours that are accepted in an organisation. As a leader, you want everyone in your organisation to feel secure and to work with colleagues with whom they are aligned, so that they give their very best to help your organisation succeed. Bullying in a team has a dramatic impact on the performance of that team and the business as a whole. Team bullying can take many different forms making it difficult to deal with. Aryanne's excellent book provides practical examples and ways to tackle team bullying which will help any organisation achieve the culture that they seek to achieve.

Paul Dickson, Chief Executive, Armstrong Watson LLP

Inclusive leadership is the key to feeling comfortable in a team, and to bringing the best of ourselves to work each day. Bullying in a team undermines this in a traumatic and diminishing way. This book sets out practical scenarios that describe a range of team bullying situations that sadly occur every day, but is also full of remedies that can address and eradicate such behaviours. It is a great addition to a manager's toolkit for enhanced performance, and for people at all levels of organisational life who need to combat team bullying.

Gillian Harford, Head of HR Strategy and Planning, AIB

As an experienced OD professional and coach who works in complex organisations, I welcome this book. I frequently encounter issues which relate to team bullying that have gone unresolved for years. Aryanne's book defines, diagnoses and offers practical strategies to address team bullying. The greatest benefit of the book is that it 'outs' the team bully and the significant detrimental impact their behaviour has inside and outside a team. Aryanne writes in a clear, no nonsense way for team members and managers alike. The book has genuine face validity, and I personally recommend it to all managers so they can health check their teams for symptoms of 'team bullying'.

Sue Holden, NHS Improvement Director

This highly accessible book is a powerful resource for those who have experienced bullying at work. They will find Aryanne Oade's analysis of how bullies operate in a team context enlightening, and feel supported by realising that their own, often highly traumatic experience, is far from unique. The book starts with a step-by-step description of how a true bully sets about enhancing their own power by attacking and under-mining a team member, whether subordinate or peer. Multiple examples and case-studies illustrate this process and underline the impact on both those targeted individually and the team as a whole.

Particularly helpful are the practical techniques for resisting bullying that are outlined in the second half of the book. Oade argues that targets can draw on their personal power to protect themselves, signalling clearly that they are not easy prey. She believes that targets, though inevitably shocked and upset, have greater control in the situation than they realise, and provides strategies for successfully resisting or derailing a bullying dynamic – even when the bully is their team manager or boss.

This book makes a valuable contribution to the literature on bullying by highlighting the role of those team members who witness or know about the bullying of one of their number. They may choose to collude with the bully, ignore the bullying behaviour, offer private support to their colleague, or stand up and actively support them. Their choices impact significantly on whether or not the bully will succeed in controlling and disempowering both individual and team. This book is highly recommended for those who have suffered from team bullying, those who seek to help them recover, and those leaders and managers whose role includes recognising and preventing this incredibly destructive aspect of organisational life.

Dr Catherine Sandler, Managing Director, Sandler Consulting

Aryanne's book on team bullying focuses on a subject that is often ignored in the workplace. Whilst there are many books on individual bullying, Aryanne's is the first to deal exclusively with team bullying. She starts by setting out how an optimal team operates before discussing in detail how to challenge bullying behaviour in a team environment. Without such effective intervention, the target's wellbeing suffers, team performance reduces and team anxiety increases. Aryanne gives clear examples throughout and allows for plenty of space within the book for personal reflection. The book guides the reader through many possible team bullying scenarios. It delivers effective strategies to help those targeted in a bully's campaign, and those in the team who witness a campaign but do not possess the tools to confront the bullying effectively. This book provides leaders of businesses with the skills they need to recognise when team bullying is occurring in their own businesses, and to take effective action using the remedies Aryanne provides.

David Kitson, Partner, Wilkins Kennedy LLP

Following her incisive critique of one-on-one bullying in the workplace, Aryanne Oade turns her attention to the psychological, social, and structural dynamics of team bullying. Her careful, compassionate, and uncompromising analysis of team bullying clearly and comprehensively exposes the conditions that enable team bullying in any work environment. By unpacking detailed scenarios and offering moments for reflection in each chapter, Oade equips employers and employees, administrators and staff, team leaders and contributors across a range of professional organisations with key tools. The book highlights the role of personal thresholds and team dynamics in fostering individual and group resilience. It describes effective ways of amassing resistance against toxic patterns, and taking collective responsibility for a healthy and sustainable workplace ecology.

Dr Cissie Fu, Dean, Faculty of Culture + Community, Emily Carr University of Art + Design

About the Author

Aryanne Oade works as a chartered psychologist, executive coach, author and publisher. She has run her coaching and development business, Oade Associates, since 1994, combining business psychology and professional acting in her projects. Aryanne coaches clients to regain their self-confidence and self-esteem after the sometimes devastating effects of team bullying. Her clients develop self-protective and self-preserving behaviour for use during any future attacks, and learn how to handle the complex dynamics involved in incidents of bullying straightforwardly and simply. Aryanne is an Associate Fellow of the British Psychological Society.

Aryanne is the bestselling author of seven previous books. She lives on a non-commercial farm in Yorkshire from where she runs her business: www.oadeassociates.com

Acknowledgements and Dedication

I want to thank several of you for allowing me to pick your brains at the start of the writing process. Due to my commitment to confidentiality, I am going to mention each of you by your first initial only. A big thank you to J, J, S and A for your generosity of spirit, for making time for me in your busy schedules, and for your willingness to share your experiences of team bullying with me. And a big thank you to A for giving me permission to use aspects of your bullying experiences in the book.

My heartfelt thanks go to June. This book was your idea. Your speedy and insightful feedback and encouragement were invaluable to me as I wrote. Thank you for your generosity, integrity and attention to detail, as well as for using your first-hand experience of team bullying in the service of the book. I firmly believe that every writer would benefit from having someone like you to work with.

Bullying in Teams is dedicated with love and admiration to HH and AF.

Note from the Author

This book focuses on the issues created for team members when one or more people in the team starts to use bullying behaviour in the team environment. In the book, I offer you, the reader, insights and tools for handling these challenging and distressing dynamics; strategies which I have honed over many years of working with clients to resolve the issues created by incidents of bullying in teams.

I hope you find the book a valuable resource from which to select tactics to help you manage the complex dynamics which play out in a team whenever one of the people in it starts to bully. However, in addition to applying the lessons from this book, you may also want to contact your employer's HR department or consult your organisation's anti-bullying policy, should these options be open to you.

In addition to reading this book, I recommend that those of you who are most impacted by experiences of bullying in your team work with a professional coach or therapist experienced in enabling recovery from experiences of bullying in a work or team environment.

Also by Aryanne Oade:

Free Yourself from Workplace Bullying:
Become Bully-Proof and Regain Control of Your Life
(Flourish 2015)

Managing Politics at Work:
The Essential Toolkit for Identifying and Managing Political
Behaviour in the Workplace
(Palgrave Macmillan 2009)

Managing Workplace Bullying:
How to Identify, Respond to and Manage Bullying Behaviour in the
Workplace (Palgrave Macmillan 2009)

Building Influence in the Workplace:
How to Gain and Retain Influence at Work
(Palgrave Macmillan 2010)

Managing Adversarial Relationships:
Operating Effectively in Relationships Characterised by
Little Trust or Support
(Palgrave Macmillan 2010)

Managing Challenging Clients:
Building Effective Relationships with Difficult Customers
(Palgrave Macmillan 2011)

Starting and Running a Coaching Business:
The Complete Guide to Setting Up and Managing a Coaching Practice
(How To Books 2008)

Detailed Chapter Contents

Introduction

An Experience of Bullying in Your Team

Perhaps you are reading this book because you or someone else in your team has been subject to bullying behaviour. The bully might have authority over you in their role as your team leader, manager or supervisor. Or maybe they are a peer or a more junior member of the team. Either way, you know that they are using unreasonable aggression in their dealings with you or other team colleagues, distressing you and creating fissures in previously effective working relationships. You can see the strain in the team that the bullying is creating as some colleagues turn a blind eye, others visibly shrink, and others again become confused and anxious. You are reading this book because you want effective input to help you manage the situation, protect yourself and your valued team connections, and confront the bullying straightforwardly and effectively.

Perhaps you are dismayed at having witnessed bullying behaviour against a colleague in your team. At the time, you couldn't find the words you needed to confront safely and effectively. You silently witnessed behaviour you found unacceptable but felt ill-equipped to tackle. Your fear was that a well-intentioned but ill-judged intervention may only make matters worse for the target and possibly for you too, escalating an already challenging situation to an unmanageable level. You wanted to confront the aggression but didn't know how to do that safely. You are reading this book because you want to find a way to confront the aggressive behaviours used by the bully in a decisive way which requires them to stop. You are looking to this book to provide you with input so you can craft a well-judged and effective set of rejoinders to bullying behaviour each and every time you witness it in the team.

Or perhaps you don't know for sure whether what you have experienced or witnessed constitutes bullying behaviour or even constitutes aggression. You are confused and self-doubting, worried that you might be over-reacting to the behaviour but also clear that what happened is troubling and disturbing. You are reading this book to find material which will enable you to decide one way or another, and to learn effective strategies for protecting yourself should a bullying attack occur in the future.

Some of you may be dismayed to recognise that you have been caught up in an incident of bullying. You didn't intend to collude with the bully, but in the moment of witnessing the attack you felt trapped, being present at a wrong-doing which you did not know how to confront. Perhaps you remained silent during an ongoing assault, seemingly giving tacit endorsement to the bullying behaviour. Or perhaps your discomfort showed in a nervous laugh or in actual verbal support of the bully, either of which leave you open to being perceived as endorsing the bullying. Disappointed by your behaviour, you are in the process of bravely confronting your own tendency towards remaining silent when you need to speak up, and want input to enable you to find a different way to handle the fear, anxiety and confusion which have lead you into this trap.

All of you are looking for guidance and practical input about how to protect your self-esteem and self-confidence in the face of bullying behaviour in your team environment. My aim in writing this book is to answer all of these questions and more by giving you access to:

- Proven strategies for handling bullying in teams.

- Effective skills to enable you to stand up to bullying in your team in a way which conclusively confronts the bully and requires them to stop.

- Empathy and compassion for the experience of being bullied in your team, and for the experience of observing other people being bullied while feeling powerless to prevent abuse from occurring.

- Knowledge about the specific ways in which bullying in a team strains previously viable working relationships, placing formerly close working bonds under duress.

- Insight into the subtle but powerful ways in which team dynamics shift when bullying behaviour is employed in a team, and how these alterations in allegiances, alliances and connections play out between team members.

- Practical wisdom to enable you to navigate your way through the confusing and changing dynamics that inevitably occur when one or more people in a team start to employ bullying methods.

- Practical input to enable you to prevent a bully from successfully grooming and targeting you in the team environment.

Why I Wrote This Book

Bullying in teams is different from one-to-one bullying. It's different because it has an impact on the entire team dynamic, creating distress for targets, altering established patterns of behaviour between colleagues who work side by side, and creating confusion among team members who have previously worked well together. It places strain on working connections and allegiances which, before the bullying commenced, were viable and rewarding. Bullying in teams calls into question the conduct of colleagues who witness bullying and do nothing about it, colleagues who tell the target that they are over-reacting when they complain about being bullied, and colleagues who turn a blind eye to the bullying in the misguided belief that this will protect them from future attack.

I am not suggesting that team bullying is either more or less harmful than one-to-one bullying. Rather, I think it creates its own set of unique dynamics, dynamics which play out slightly differently in each team affected by bullying. A team in which the team leader is the bully will be affected in ways which are distinct from a team in which a more junior member is the bully. A small team of four or five people where everyone works closely together may find that all its relationships are placed under strain by the presence of bullying behaviour in the team environment. A larger team of fifteen may find that the impact of bullying is dissipated for the majority of team members but felt most keenly by those personally targeted by the bullying. But in all these cases, the strain is very real both for the targets and for those who work alongside them. What each of you needs is a resource which will show you what team bullying is, how it is likely to affect the dynamics in your team, and how to handle these circumstances in an effective way so that the bullying is confronted and the team preserved. This is exactly what this book will do.

This book is written to 'you' the reader, but it will also be of value to those of you who are involved in responding to alleged incidents of team bullying in your role as human resources or dignity at work advisors, as strategists and policy formulators, and as coaches who work with clients resolving these issues.

What This Book Will Do for You

This book represents a synthesis of proven, powerful techniques from the evidence base of psychology. The material in the book will enable you to acquire practical strategies through which to protect your inner self from the impact of bullying behaviour in the team environment, preserving your self-esteem, self-belief and self-confidence. It will also help you to develop insight and wisdom about the nature of the dynamic that the bully is trying to create in their interactions with you and your team colleagues. Importantly, it will challenge you to review how you currently *behave* in the face of bullying aggression and to develop new and more effective behaviours for use at these times. These new behaviours will simultaneously protect you *and* send back an unequivocal message to the bully that you will not be a straightforward person for them to target, nor will you stand by and remain passive, silent and still while you observe bullying in the team.

This book will describe the chaos, confusion and damage which is done to previously effective team relationships when one or more people in the team start to use bullying behaviour. It will describe the strain and fractures that evolve in previously enjoyable and rewarding working connections when bullying behaviour causes the dynamics in the team to alter. Absorbing the learning from this book will provide you with know-how and skills through which to address the confusion and muddle which can arise in your most valued team relationships as your colleagues withdraw, close down, push you away or resort to other unhelpful strategies as they struggle to cope with the presence of bullying behaviour in the team.

The case studies and cameos in this book will provide you with knowledge and insight into why bullies bully, what they want to achieve by using these methods in a team environment and how to confront bullying behaviour effectively. They will address worries you may have of unintentional collusion with bullying behaviour simply because you don't know how to stand up to it safely.

Applying the lessons from this book will enable you to develop your ability to:

- Protect yourself from team bullying at the time of an attack.

- Understand the ways in which your team's work, performance and productivity are likely to be undermined due to the presence of bullying behaviour in the team environment.

- Gain the confidence, skills and resilience you need to confront bullying behaviour in your team safely and effectively.

- Provide much-needed life-enhancing support to a team colleague subject to bullying behaviour.

- Change your own approach so that the next time you witness bullying in your team you can avoid the pitfalls of active or passive collusion and confront the wrong-doing straightforwardly and simply.

My wish for you as you read this book is that it provides you with input and resources through which to feel less intimidated by bullying behaviour, better equipped to resist it, and more able to protect yourself should you be unfortunate enough to be targeted by a bully or witness bullying behaviour in your team.

My Experience of Helping Clients to Detoxify from Experiences of Team Bullying

I have coached and worked with many clients over the past twenty-five years whose experience of their team has altered dramatically as a result of bullying behaviour. I have also coached and worked with many people who have witnessed bullying taking place in their team, who did not feel equipped to do anything about it. Worried that if they tried to confront the wrong-doing they'd make themselves a ready target for the bully, they usually observed what was happening with a sinking heart and growing sense of powerlessness and frustration.

As part of each coaching process, I ask my client to step back from the experience of being subject to or a witness to bullying in their team. I ask them to relate to me the most challenging circumstances they have faced, the ones in which the bullying was the most destructive to them or other people. I then recreate these dynamics using the services of one of my professional actor colleagues in a series of enacted scenarios. During these scenarios, my clients put themselves back into the abusive situation in the safety of the coaching room. They learn how to handle the dynamics in way which is self-protective and self-preserving, and which allows them to retain control in an abusive situation. They learn to express their own personal power and confront bullies effectively. Using simple and straightforward techniques they learn to manage behaviours which previously left them feeling abused or powerless.

The techniques I describe in this book come out of my work in helping many clients to develop the skills, mind-set and know-how they need to handle bullying behaviour effectively. In writing this book I am not intending to provide you with prescriptive instructions about how to handle your own situation, but rather to describe to you what has proved effective for my clients so that you can consider how best to apply this to your own situation. It is my hope that along with my clients you will discover levels of inner resilience, self-belief and self-confidence that you did not know you possessed, resources which will enable you to confront workplace bullying and prevent yourself and your colleagues from being subject to further attack.

How to Get Best Value from This Book

I have written this book with a clear principle in mind. This principle is that I consider the use of bullying behaviour to be the responsibility of the bully 100% of the time, with no exceptions. For those of you with current or previous experience of being bullied, this means that you did not do, say or feel anything which provoked the aggression you were subject to. Rather, the bully resorted to bullying methods *because of pre-existing issues in their own life that you are not responsible for.*

Consequently, this book will encourage you to make a clear distinction between what you *are* responsible for – using self-protective behaviour at the time of an attack – and what you are *not* responsible for – being bullied and the bully's use of aggression. Being vulnerable to grooming and bullying does not mean that you are to blame for being bullied. That responsibility rests wholly with the bully.

This book will encourage you to:

- Reflect on your experiences to identify bullying behaviour in your team.

- Adopt a self-protective and self-preserving mind-set should you be targeted or should you witness an attack.

- Select effective methods of confronting the bullying while also retaining control in the moment of the attack.

- Recognise why these tactics will be effective in protecting you, while also sending a clear message to the bully that you will not be an easy person for them to target.

- Understand the bullying dynamic that the bully wants to create in your team, so that you can be better prepared to handle it effectively.

- Recognise what to do should you witness bullying in the team so that you don't become a passive enabler or active colluder with the abuse.

- Develop your ability to offer valuable support to someone who is being targeted either at the time of an attack, or shortly afterwards.

Longer Case Studies and Shorter Examples

Throughout the book you will find realistic case studies and shorter examples of bullying in a team environment. Some of these case studies and cameos represent an anonymised version of a real-life situation which a client or contact of mine has given me permission to include in the book. Other scenarios are a blend of a number of incidents which I have synthesised and anonymised into one case to produce a fictional but realistic example. A minority of the examples are entirely fictional but based on real-life dynamics. Due to my commitment to absolute permanent confidentiality for each of my clients and contacts, I have written the real-life examples in a way which fully protects the identities of those involved.

Each case study and shorter example highlights:

- The behaviours and tactics used by the bully in the team environment depicted in the scenario.

- How these behaviours impact the target and other members of the team.

- Ways in which the team dynamics and relationships are altered as a result of the bullying, both at the time of the attack and subsequently.

From Chapter 4 onwards, each case study and shorter example will also highlight:

- Effective responses which the target and other team members could employ to protect themselves at the time of an attack and prevent a bullying dynamic being inculcated into the team.

Your Journey to a Healthier Team Dynamic

I hope you find this book invaluable as you come to terms with your experiences of bullying behaviour in your team. I trust that absorbing its messages will deepen your understanding of how bullying has altered the relationships and allegiances in your team, how it has created a level of complexity in the team dynamic that wasn't present before, and how to counteract instances of bullying in a decisive way. Above all, I trust that distilling the learning from the book will enable you to become bully-proof against future attack.

With my very best wishes

Aryanne Oade

C. Psychol.

Chapter 1
What is Team Bullying?

The Character of Your Team

Your team is unique. It is composed of different people each of whom brings to work specific values, skills, knowledge, personal qualities and beliefs. Your team consists of a framework of allegiances, alliances, and both formal and informal connections which enable different people to work together productively, get along with one another as much as is needed in the workplace, and focus on the joint accomplishment of tasks to be completed. Each of you contributes to the team culture in a slightly different way creating a team environment which can be enjoyable and rewarding, which can be a source of strain or which can even be destructive to some of you.

Before we explore the impact of team bullying on team dynamics, let's set the scene by describing how a healthy effective team operates. In this ideal scenario, the way the team leader uses their authority is key to the effectiveness of the team and cannot be underestimated. An effective leader has a suite of styles from which they select, depending on the person they are working with and the issues to be addressed. Their aim is to bring the best out of everyone in the team, while making sure that the work is done to standard and on time. However, it is not only the way the leader behaves which has a bearing on the atmosphere in the team. The way that each team member conducts themselves day-to-day is important too. In an effective team, the leader and the team members work hard to:

- Handle confrontation and conflict in an open and transparent way, seeking to make difference a point of growth and collaboration rather than a point of division and unresolved tension.

- Actively co-operate with one another when there is disagreement about a goal, method or process in order to find a solution which addresses the underlying issues.

- Clarify team objectives as well as individual goals so that everyone considers that the work they are doing is valuable or necessary.

- Demonstrate trusting and supportive behaviour towards one another even when there is tension and strain.

- Employ decision-making and problem-solving processes which enable everyone who wants to make a contribution to an issue to do so simply and straightforwardly.

- Develop their skills and knowledge so they don't stagnate or become bored.

You may or may not recognise these characteristics of a healthy effective team from your experience of your own team day-to-day. But as a member of a team, your role involves finding a way to work productively alongside your colleagues, some of whom may have been there longer than you, some of whom may carry more organisational authority than you or may have mastered different skills to you, and some of whom may have such different values to you that, if it weren't for the work you do together, you might not easily find anything to talk about. However, under normal circumstances, you want to work effectively with everyone else, even if that proves a challenge from time to time.

The ideal is that everyone in your team gives their best, contributes in ways that they find professionally and personally rewarding and uses their skills to enable the team to achieve more with them than without them. By making a skilled contribution, you become a productive member of the team, someone more likely to receive positive feedback, feel appreciated and feel that you belong. In order to do these things consistently, you need to establish and maintain three distinct but related contracts with your team. Let's explore them.

Your Three Contracts with Your Team

Your Work Contract

On joining a team, there are specific practical boundaries that you agree to abide by. You agree to arrive on time and, in return, you expect to get paid on time. You agree to utilise your skills, stamina and energy to meet the goals of your role and you expect to be given work you are qualified to do. You agree to work to the required standard within the required timescale and you expect to be promoted on merit. You recognise that you will work well with some of your colleagues, and less well with others. Your team will contain some people with whom you form work-based friendships, some with whom you work well but don't have a friendship, and others, again, with whom you have no shared values and little in common but whom you find ways to work with anyway. You trust that, by and large, you will all seek to work productively with one another within the boundaries of your work contracts, focusing on the tasks at hand, whether or not you share similar views and opinions on non-work topics and issues.

Your Relational Contract

On joining a team, you implicitly agree to abide by certain norms of behaviour. This relational contract means that you agree to respect a pre-existing set of values which enable disparate people from possibly divergent ethnic, cultural and social backgrounds to work productively side-by-side. These norms of behaviour represent a culture of customs, conventions and unspoken understandings that keep your team relationships viable and make the accomplishment of the work feasible.

Having joined the team, you may decide that you either like or dislike these established norms, and assuming you like them enough to commit to the team, you may try to influence some aspects of the culture towards areas which you find more welcome and less bothersome. When you and your colleagues find ways of working together that are productive for everyone in the team, your combined energies, commitment and skills can be fully utilised in achieving the goals of the team, creating top quality outcomes and an enjoyable working process for all of you.

Your Psychological Contract

Your psychological contract with your team operates in a different way. It means that you expect to be safe while you are at work unless you have chosen to do a job which entails obvious specified risks like the hazards willingly and knowingly incurred by members of the armed forces or mining engineers or deep-sea divers. Assuming that your role does not entail occupational hazards, in the normal course of your work you would not expect relational, psychological or emotional threat or danger. You expect to go to work in your team and be relationally, psychologically and emotionally safe, so that you can use your personal resources and professional attributes to perform your role to the best of your ability, rather than having to use your energies to protect yourself.

When bullying behaviour is introduced into a team environment by one or more members of that team, your psychological contract is likely to be compromised as you start to feel anxious and unsafe. But, depending on the severity and length of the campaign against you, all three of your contracts could become compromised.

So, what is team bullying and how does it differ from aggressive non-bullying behaviour? Let's explore those two issues during the remainder of this chapter, starting with an exploration of what constitutes team bullying.

A Definition of Team Bullying

Team bullying involves:

- One-off, sporadic or frequent personal attacks against you by a member of your team when you are alone or in a team setting.

- A deliberate attempt by the bully to undermine your ability to carry out your work, or to injure your reputation with your team colleagues, and/or to weaken your self-esteem, self-confidence and self-belief.

- A deliberate attempt by the bully to remove personal power, reputational influence and/or organisational status from you and retain that control for themselves.

- An alteration in the team dynamic as energy is diverted away from work and towards handling the distress of being targeted, the strain created between colleagues, and the need to protect yourselves from future attack.

I consider that all four elements in the above definition need to be present simultaneously for any incident to be a true team bullying. I think this holds true whether the behaviour involved is subtle and indirect, such as the bully whispering falsehoods about you when you are not in the room to undermine your reputation, or more clear and obvious such as an aggressive verbal assault launched by a bully against you during a one-to-one encounter or a team meeting to undermine your self-esteem.

Consider the following short examples:

- A frank IT team member in a busy marketing firm attends a meeting of her nine hard-working peers. Her nine peers are all conscientious, quiet technicians, none of whom is as verbally direct as the IT team member. In the middle of the meeting, she suddenly and unexpectedly snaps. Standing up, she shouts loudly, telling her colleagues that they are incompetent and lazy, and declares that she is the one doing all the work. She then stomps towards the drinks trolley, where she proceeds to pour herself a coffee, her face visibly contorted with rage. Her colleagues watch immobilised with shock and amazement, remaining still and silent when she retakes her place at the table. For the remainder of the meeting, each of the mild-mannered peers avoids eye contact with the IT team member and, head down, speaks as little as possible, enabling her to steer the meeting wherever she wants it to go. In the coming days, the peers walk on eggshells around the IT team member. They worry about when the next attack will take place, what form it will take and how they will handle it. Some of them experience trouble concentrating and can't seem to apply themselves to their work as they normally would.

- A junior doctor on a geriatric ward is reviewing patient notes at the end of a tiring day. On three previous occasions he has discovered small but important errors in some patients' notes, mistakes which he attributed to the nursing team in charge of records. On each occasion that he had noticed an error, the junior doctor had made a point of going to the nurses' station and pointing it out to the nurses on duty. On noticing a similar error for the fourth time, the junior doctor throws his arms up in fury and strides over to the nurses' station. He rages at the nurse who is seated there, berating her loudly for failing patients, calling her a disgrace and telling her that she shouldn't be allowed anywhere near vulnerable patients. The nurse is stunned. During the remainder of that week she replays the incident over and over in her mind, and tells every other nurse working the day-shift about it in an attempt to process what happened and find closure. She discusses the possibility of confronting the doctor but decides against it, concerned that he might not apologise. She remains intimidated and anxious every time she sees him on the ward or attends to one of the patients, each of whom must have heard what the doctor said. Other nurses who work alongside the doctor remain wary of him, keeping their patient-related discussions with him as short as possible.

Let's apply the definition to these examples to see if they constitute incidents of team bullying. In the first case, the IT team member directs her tirade at her peer group during a team meeting. Is this an example of team bullying? Yes, it is. It fulfils all four aspects of the definition. Let's examine them one by one:

- Firstly, the IT team member's attack is personally directed at her entire peer group during a team meeting. She insults their professionalism by calling them 'incompetent'. She insults them personally by labelling them 'lazy', and she elevates herself to a superior position over them by claiming that she is the one doing 'all the work'. She attacks all nine of her peers at the same time, a tactic that is designed to demonstrate the degree of contempt she holds for them.

- Secondly, her verbal attack is directed at the self-esteem and self-confidence of her peer group both as persons and as profes-sionals. She attacks them all simultaneously, applying the same derogatory remarks to all of them. Her verbal attack is designed to

14

undermine the self-esteem of each of her peers, to cause to them to doubt their individual contribution to their joint work, and to place doubt into the minds of each peer about the value of everyone else's contribution.

- Thirdly, the IT team member's attack is entirely about power. Choosing to take advantage of her greater force of personality compared to her colleagues', she chooses a specific form of attack which the more understated and conflict-averse technicians find hard to combat. In attacking them in that specific way, she wants to remove power from each of them as an individual, and from the group as a whole, and retain that control for herself. Her attack is calculated to undermine the personal power, reputational influence and organisational status of each peer and retain that power for herself.

- Fourthly, energy from the team *is* diverted away from its work towards coping with the bullying both at the time of the attack and subsequently. To the mild-mannered and conflict-averse technicians, the IT team member's attack is completely counter-cultural, unexpected and frightening. Members of that team simply do not speak to one another in such an explosive and aggressive way. The peers have few obvious coping strategies for handling such a powerful assault, and each of them worries about what happened, why it happened and the potential for a recurrence. Their individual and collective mind is not on their work for the remainder of that meeting, nor subsequently when they struggle to speak openly with the IT team member. Whether the IT team member will succeed in her plan to take control away from her peer group remains to be seen, but she has undoubtedly altered the team dynamic away from carefree co-operation towards reduced team effectiveness as each peer struggles with their anxiety and confusion.

In the second example, a junior doctor who notices a repeated error in his patients' notes, storms over to the nurses' station and launches a verbal assault on the nurse who is seated there. Is this an example of team bullying or is this a meticulous junior doctor safeguarding patient care? Let's apply the four-part definition to find out.

- Does the junior doctor orchestrate a personal attack on the nurse seated at the nurses' station? Yes, he does. He attacks the nurse without warning in full view of the ward. He attacks her without knowing if she has had anything to do with the particular error that has come to his attention. He attacks her without there being any immediate danger to a patient, or any context that he knows about that could justify such an egregious verbal assault. His attack is deeply personal as he ragingly accuses her of being a disgrace and someone who is failing her patients.

- Does he deliberately try to undermine the nurse's ability to carry out her work, injure her reputation, and/or undermine her self-esteem and self-confidence? Yes, he does all three of these things. The junior doctor's attack is calculated to encourage the nurse to think she is woeful at what she does. He specifically says that she should not be around vulnerable patients. Because his raging attack is carried out suddenly, he gives the nurse no time to protect herself. She is completely vulnerable, seated alone at the nurses' station, and will likely feel humiliated professionally and personally by the wording and power of an assault conducted in full view of the patients she is there to care for. Knowing that the patients on the ward have heard what is said is particularly painful for the nurse. From that moment onwards, every time she attends to a patient she wonders what they think of her and whether they agree with the doctor's assessment of her work.

- Does the junior doctor do this in a deliberate attempt to remove personal power, reputational influence and/or organisational status from the nurse and retain this power for himself? Yes, absolutely. He primarily attacks her reputation in the eyes of patients, and her organisational status as a nurse. But the force of his attack leaves the nurse reeling, and impacts her personal power too as she is unable to defend herself or find anything to say at the time of the attack. As a junior doctor, her assailant possesses greater organisational authority than she does, which makes his verbal comments all the more castigating. He attacks her without warning in full view of their patients, calling her a disgrace and not fit to be near vulnerable people. His words and actions undermine her reputation in the eyes of patients overhearing the assault.

- Do the junior doctor's actions cause the nurse's energy to be diverted away from her work, and does it impact the nursing team's work and relationships subsequently? Yes, both of these things happen. The tenor of the attack puts fear and anxiety into the nurse's mind causing her to feel acute discomfort when she thinks about it. Understandably, she talks to other members of the nursing team to try to process what has happened, causing some of their energy to be diverted away from their tasks and towards supporting her. Each of these members of the nursing team becomes nervous at the prospect of working with the junior doctor, and as a result each of them tries to curtail the length of their patient-related discussions with him. We don't know if patient care is affected by their desire to have as little to do with him as possible, but we can be sure that none of the nurses trusts him in the same way as before his egregious attack on their nursing colleague. Even if the junior doctor does want to safeguard patient care, this is no way to go about it as his actions have directly injured a member of the nursing staff and left him vulnerable to a charge of team bullying.

In both of these examples, all four elements of the definition of team bullying are fulfilled simultaneously, even though the dynamics are quite different across the two instances. In both cases, the bully attacks their targets personally, professionally and reputationally. In both cases, the bully's objective is to remove power from their targets and retain that control for themselves. In both cases the energy of the target and their team is taken away from their work. Instead they invest energy in reviewing what happened, identifying coping strategies they could use should there be a further attack, and attempting to lessen the level of anxiety they feel about working alongside a team bully.

Your Power: The Team Bully's Battleground

You'll have noticed that the third bullet in the definition refers to three forms of power. A true team bully wants to remove power from you, and might target your personal power, reputational influence and/or organisational status. A skilled team bully wants to reduce your sense of your own effectiveness as a person and as a professional, and injure your credibility in the eyes of team colleagues and contacts. Let's explore these three forms of power.

Your Personal Power

This is your personal right to choose how you behave, what you believe, think and feel (especially about yourself), and what choices you make at work. It involves your right to decide where you place the boundaries in your relationships. A true team bully wants to take these choices away from you, limiting the options available to you at the time of an attack, while also reducing your sense of control over your behaviour during that attack and, if possible, subsequently as well. The more the bully succeeds at limiting your choices, the more they can injure your inner self: your self-esteem, your self-confidence and your self-belief – and, in an adult, all of these are predicated to some extent on being able to choose your behaviour, thoughts, feelings and beliefs.

Your Reputational Influence

This is the credibility you have with your team colleagues due to their respect for you as a person, their respect for the standard of your work, the quality of your skills and the input you give to team meetings. This form of power *is* your reputation as a member of the team, and it comes from the quality of relationship you maintain with your team colleagues. A true team bully will take actions which injure your credibility in the eyes of your colleagues. Their methods may include lying about you to discredit you, slandering you to cause other people to question their faith in you, or exaggerating small errors and misjudgements you have made to drop the thought into colleagues' minds that you are not up to your job and are not quite the person they thought you were. A true team bully may also take steps to exclude you from team social situations, limiting the contact you might have with colleagues who, in the normal course of events, you would expect to have a coffee or lunch with. The resultant social isolation and exclusion can be more painful than the bullying itself, causing you to doubt yourself and feel terribly alone at a time when you sorely need support.

Your Organisational Status

This is the authority that goes with your role and relates to your position as supervisor, manager or team leader, and also relates to your role as a subject matter expert. A team bully wants to reduce the authority you exert over team affairs and may target your organisational status to achieve this aim. Whether you are a team leader and the bully is one of your team members, or whether the bully is your peer, they may attack your judgement to undermine your authority, suggesting that you are not fit to carry out your duties or that you lack the skills to do your job well. These attacks on your judgement and skills may occur in team meetings in full view of everyone else. They may occur in one-to-one meetings between the two of you, or behind your back when you are not present to hear what is said and cannot defend yourself. By targeting your authority, the bully is hoping that you will relinquish some or all of it to them, reducing your level of influence in the team and giving the bully room to take over some or all of your work. By repeatedly targeting your level of skill, the bully is also hoping that you *will* start to doubt your own ability and competence, so that you *do* start to make mistakes and misjudgements, and perhaps even fail to reach your performance targets. Should this happen, they can then step in and take over, seizing kudos and prestige for 'saving the day'.

Skilled team bullies will target all three forms of power within the same campaign, simultaneously attacking your inner self, your relationships, and your ability to handle your authority and carry out your duties. A campaign orchestrated by a skilled team bully can have an overwhelming impact. It can leave you reeling under a triple whammy of abuse aimed at your personhood, your reputation and your livelihood.

Being Intermittently Nice: A Team Bully's Ploy to Create Confusion

As well as targeting your personal power, relationships and status, a skilled team bully may also seek to throw you off guard by periodically being nice to you. You may find that when you are alone together, the bully smiles and behaves warmly towards you. Or they may perform apparent acts of kindness, like making you a cup of tea in full view of the rest of the team. These instances are designed to confuse you, creating self-doubt as you become unsure whether you are misjudging the bully. Incidents like these can render you more vulnerable to a subsequent attack as your self-doubt results in you failing to brace yourself sufficiently swiftly the next time you encounter the bully.

These examples of apparent kindness also make it more challenging for other people in the team to believe that you are being targeted, especially if the bullying only occurs in one-to-one meetings between you and the bully.

Consider these short examples:

- The member of a skilled engineering team starts to bully three of his peers. He employs a combination of snide and cutting comments to their faces in one-to-one meetings, while also making demeaning and derisory comments about them behind their backs. Two weeks into his campaign, at a point when all three team members are discomforted by his aggression, he drives into the company car park and notices one of them seated in his car reading his emails. All smiles and bonhomie, the bullying peer rushes over to his colleague's car, signalling that he should wind down the window so they can chat. The team member is disoriented and confused. In the split second that he experiences his bullying peer's apparently genuine friendliness, he doubts whether he has previously judged him correctly. He makes the mistake of lowering his window and, in so doing, lowers his guard as well. He is met with a short period of warmth and charm, before his bullying peer tells him in a curt and cold manner that he has more important things to do than spend the day chatting to the likes of him. He then turns smartly on his heels and briskly walks off towards the office building, leaving his team colleague feeling punctured and even more confused than before.

- A team supervisor in an insurance firm bullies one member of his team while favouring selected others. The entire team works in one office, seated at individual workstations positioned around a large square table. The target is a quiet and unassuming young woman who is diligent and hardworking. Her team supervisor's campaign leaves her feeling self-doubting and alone, as no one else in the team seems to notice when she is subject to his castigating and derogatory remarks. Indeed, when he is targeting her in full view of them, her team colleagues keep their heads down and carry on with their work, behaving as if nothing untoward is happening. On her birthday, the team supervisor arrives with a tray of small cakes and makes a big show of presenting them to 'the birthday girl', telling her to decide which cake to give to which team member. She is horrified at being told to do this, a command he issues while standing over her shoulder. She hates being in a spotlight at the best of times, but having him stand over her and enjoy her discomfort is appalling for her. Totally confused at the invidious position he has placed her in, and faced with the prospect of having to dole out cakes to the same people who silently witness attacks on her, the hardworking target looks blankly at the team supervisor and withdraws her hands under her desk, wishing the ground would open up and swallow her.

Let's analyse these two examples to see what lessons we can draw from them. In the first instance, the bully takes advantage of an impromptu encounter with one of his targets in the company car park. Seizing the moment, he approaches him full of warmth and apparent good humour, gesturing to him to lower his car window and have a chat. The target is nonplussed but doesn't want to appear rude, so he does lower his window and, in that moment, sets himself up for another incident of team bullying. He stays in the car, lowers the window and becomes vulnerable. In the short exchange which follows, the bully is initially nice to his target but, out of the blue, turns on him in a cold and cutting attack in which he tells him that he hasn't got time to talk to the likes of him, before walking off in a self-important manner. The key lesson here, is that the target allowed himself to become vulnerable *because he did not want to be rude* and because he misinterpreted the bully's warm overtures as genuine, rather than *seeing them for the rouse they were*. Instead of bracing himself for another encounter with the bully, the target doubted whether this apparently genuinely warm man could really be bullying him, and became subject to another incident in an escalating campaign. We will return to this example at the start of Chapter 7 which focuses on peer bullying, to examine what the target could have done to protect himself effectively from his peer's bullying overture to wind down the window and chat.

In the second example, the calculating and cynical team supervisor escalates his campaign against his hardworking team member in full view of everyone else in the team, using her birthday as a rouse to humiliate and confuse her. He brings in a tray of cakes in apparent celebration of her birthday. But the thinly veiled ploy is really another opportunity to humiliate her as he tells her to decide which colleague will receive which cake, a task which places her in an embarrassing position, while he stands over her enjoying her discomfort. She is so confused by this dishonest celebration of her birthday by a man who is bullying her, and by his command to select which cake will go to which colleague, that she stares blankly at him. Her decision to place her hands underneath the desk does at least give him a clear signal that she won't be played with like that, and preserves some of her dignity, but she still has to endure his blatant attempt to patronise and manipulate her on her birthday. The key lesson here is that the team supervisor carries out this charade partly *for the benefit of the other members of the team.* He calculates that, since all of them passively accept his bullying of the hardworking young woman, failing to offer her support at the time or afterwards, he can be fairly sure that his apparent act of kindness towards her will also meet with their silent collusion. His 'celebration of her birthday' is calculated to make it very difficult for her to complain about his bullying behaviour as he would cite it as a clear example of how positive his attitude is towards her. Knowing that the team silently endorse his bullying means that he can be fairly certain they will back him up if there is an internal enquiry and report that, indeed, he did bring cakes into the office on her birthday.

In each case, the dynamics surrounding the apparent act of kindness displayed by the bully are different. But in both cases, the bully's actions are insincere and self-serving. In the first instance, the bully's warmth creates sufficient self-doubt that the target unwisely lowers his car window and is subject to another attack. In the second instance, the bully's birthday celebration enables the devious team supervisor to simultaneously patronise his target while also undermining her credibility if she ever does make a complaint against him.

Let's now resume our exploration of what does and what does not constitute team bullying by examining how to tell the difference between a true team bully and a colleague who is aggressive but non-bullying.

Aggression in Your Team: The Difference Between Aggressive Non-Bullying Behaviour and True Team Bullying

There is a world of difference between aggressive non-bullying behaviour and true team bullying. The difference lies in the *intention of the team member using the aggression*. True team bullying is about power. The team bully wants to remove power from you and retain that control for themselves. This is distinct from the aggressive colleague who is not a bully. That person is unable to manage their own emotion that day and lets it spill over into their dealings with you. This colleague is *not trying to remove power* from you when they speak or behave aggressively. What they *are* doing is mishandling their own emotional expression, something which in no way excuses them from behaving in an aggressive manner. Neither does it obviate their need to learn how to handle their own emotion far better. Nor does it remove from them the need to learn a greater range of emotional intelligence skills for use with you and their other colleagues. But it does exonerate them from the charge of being a true team bully.

That said, the impact of their aggression on you can still be highly distressing. Those of you who feel intimidated or vulnerable to aggression may find just one incident of aggressive non-bullying behaviour to be one too many. Depending on how it is handled, that one incident could result in damage to your relational or psychological contract with your team and, in some cases, could result in you wanting the aggressive colleague to work in another team so you don't have to face further unpalatable anger. But for our purposes here, unless your colleague was deliberately targeting you to remove power from you, I wouldn't consider their behaviour to be true team bullying. They certainly need frank feedback on their behaviour. They need to take responsibility for their use of aggression in the team environment, and cease doing it. They need to apologise. But, if your colleague didn't want to remove at least one form of power from you, then no matter how reprehensible and upsetting their behaviour toward you, they did not use bullying behaviour.

In this chapter, we have explored a number of themes while examining what constitutes team bullying. Let's now illustrate those themes in more detail in a longer example.

Case Study 1: Bullying Boss

A busy news desk at a daily paper employs six journalists who are seated in a straight line, each with their own workstation and computer. Their news editor sits opposite them, centrally located in a strategic position from which he can observe each member of his team at work. One of the reporters on his team is a recently widowed mother of three young children. Known for her principled journalism and vibrant writing style, she specialises in newsworthy political stories. During her first six months of work on the news desk, the political reporter gets on well with the new news editor. He regularly assigns her challenging stories to research and write up and, due to her extensive and well-developed contacts among community and government leaders, as well as in political circles, her pieces are well received by the news editor and the readers of the paper.

One Wednesday afternoon, a supplier to the paper comes into the newsroom to sell a selection of cuddly toys. The political reporter buys a small bear for her youngest son, a camel for her younger daughter and a giraffe for her elder daughter. Feeling light-hearted and pleased at doing something fun for her children, the political reporter shows the toys to the news editor. He thinks the giraffe is particularly nice and asks the political reporter to go and buy one for him. She agrees to do just that but, by the time she tracks down the supplier in an adjoining office, he has sold out of giraffes. She tells the news editor that there are no giraffes left and is surprised when he looks her in the eye and says: 'In that case, I'll have yours'. The political reporter tells him that she wants her daughter to have the giraffe as that animal is her favourite. Unmoved, the news editor repeats that he wants the giraffe she has already bought and holds his right palm out, waiting for the political reporter to hand the toy to him.

From that moment, the news editor's attitude to the reporter changes dramatically. He permanently cold shoulders her, veering between being unfriendly and actively hostile. When the news editor enters the newsroom, he says hello to everyone in it except the political reporter. Avoiding eye contact with her, he smiles and chats with everyone else, resolutely ignoring her. He also ignores her at all other times, behaving as if she isn't in the room. Initially confused by his sudden change of behaviour, the political reporter tries several times to break the ice by saying 'hello' to him and smiling. On each occasion, the news editor either completely ignores her or turns his back on her, grunting something unintelligible as he walks away.

Over the next few weeks, the news editor extends his campaign against the political reporter. His usual way of assigning work to his team members is via email, sending each person three jobs to follow up on. He ceases sending any jobs to the political reporter, leaving her sitting at her desk unproductive and excluded from the work of the team while everyone else is busy with their tasks. Frustrated, she starts to search the internet looking for stories to pursue. The news editor observes her doing this, and fires a single lead into her email inbox. The political news editor is so engrossed with her internet research that she doesn't notice the email from the news editor. She is dismayed when, only five minutes after sending it to her, the news editor strides over to her workstation to tell her that he is taking the lead back and reassigning it 'because you can't even be bothered to read it!'

Over the next nine months, the news editor does not assign a single job to the political reporter. Everyone in the team recognises that the political reporter is being cold shouldered and excluded from work assignments, but most of them remain passive in the face of the bullying and don't say or do anything about it, either at the time of an incident or subsequently. Each of these passive colleagues spends more time by themselves at their desks, doesn't socialise around the office as much as they normally would, and finds it difficult to concentrate for long periods of time. However, a couple of the team members do speak privately with the political reporter, commiserating with her and offering what support they can out of the earshot of the news editor. One of them tells the political reporter that she isn't the first person the news editor has treated this way, that in recent years several reporters, all female, have been targeted by him, and that each eventually chose to leave the newspaper because 'once the news editor doesn't like you, you are doomed.'

Then the news editor escalates his campaign further by making a series of unfounded allegations against the political reporter to his editor. The political reporter is called into the editor's office to explain why she has let her writing standards drop, why she doesn't follow up on leads the news editor sends to her, why she is consistently late for work and why she appears disinterested in the work of the news desk. The political reporter does her best to defend herself from these bogus accusations, none of which has any basis in fact. The editor does not interrupt her while she speaks, but he does not believe her either, having already decided that the reports provided to him by the news editor are entirely factual.

As the campaign against her progresses, the political news editor becomes more and more distressed at the thought of going to work. Her sleep becomes fitful and shallow. She dreads the thought of leaving the house each morning. As she approaches the newspaper's offices, her palms become clammy, she starts to shake and her anxiety levels rise. She dreads opening the newsroom door and seeing the news editor in the room. She feels a potent and debilitating combination of powerlessness, anger and fury at the injustice of being bullied, and starts to slide into a depression. Her distress is compounded by the news editor's habit of treating her with warmth and good humour whenever the editor or the publisher enters the newsroom. His sudden friendliness on these occasions is completely out of keeping with his behaviour towards her at all other times.

Ten months into the campaign, and after the political reporter has made two unsuccessful attempts to be re-assigned to work for a different news editor, the newspaper organises a drinks party after work for the city community leaders. The political reporter has a positive relationship with many of the community leaders, and one of them seeks her out during the evening. He tells her that he has just been speaking with the news editor who told him that he hates the political reporter and 'wants to end her career'. The reporter is horrified at the degree of malice and vengefulness that the news editor reserves for her. She has been at the newspaper for many years, is a single mother, and doesn't want to lose her job. But faced with this level of unremitting malevolence, she decides that she must act.

She consults a lawyer but, after discussions about the time and effort it will take to mount a law suit, decides not to go ahead. Exhausted from having to defend herself from unjust accusations of underperformance, fatigued from dealing with bullying behaviour for nearly a year, and ground down by having to cope with the challenging symptoms of distress she is experiencing, the political reporter decides to leave the newspaper. She tells the news editor that unless he writes her a superb reference, she will sue him. The news editor knows that there are several other ex-employees of the newspaper who could join the political reporter in filing a joint action against him. Faced with the prospect of going to court or writing a glowing reference, he does the latter.

The political reporter leaves the newspaper and quickly finds employment with a rival publication, albeit it takes her a long time to recover her composure and well-being following the devastating campaign against her.

Bullying Boss: Analysing the Team Dynamics

Let's examine the dynamics which play out between the news editor, the political reporter and the wider newspaper team. We will do this using the four-part definition of team bullying introduced earlier in the chapter as the context for the analysis.

Firstly, does the news editor orchestrate a personal attack on the political reporter? Yes, certainly he does. The incident which signals the start of his campaign is highly personal to the political reporter as it involves gifts she has bought for her children. But it is the way in which the news editor targets her personally during the campaign that is so pernicious. Employing a combination of misogyny and status consciousness, the news editor's main tactic against his target is to deny that she is in the room. He refuses to acknowledge her presence. He ignores her. He grunts when she speaks to him. He excludes her from work assignments. He doesn't look at her. He treats her *as if she isn't there.* These are all deeply punishing, personally-targeted assaults. By denying her existence, the news editor targets the political reporter's personhood: her sense of self. He adds further insult to injury by suddenly becoming friendly and warm whenever one of his bosses enters the room. This tactic is particularly galling for the political reporter. She endures a mocking show of humanity from a man whose personal attacks on her demonstrate a degree of heartlessness towards a recently widowed mother of three young children.

Does the news editor deliberately try to undermine the political reporter's ability to carry out her work, injure her reputation, and/or undermine her self-esteem and self-confidence? Absolutely. He does all three of these things. Firstly, he attacks her ability to carry out her work by failing to assign her any leads to follow up on, while continuing to assign jobs to all the other reporters in the team. This strategy leaves the political reporter out of the team's work, excludes her from her own duties, and leaves her frustrated and alone. Secondly, the news editor injures the political reporter's reputation by lying about her to the editor. He makes up a series of false allegations about her performance and conduct to undermine her credibility in the eyes of the editor. The news editor does this for two reasons: to smear her reputation and to cover his own tracks. If he can convince the editor that the political reporter is under-performing and handling herself poorly, it is unlikely that the editor will listen to any complaints she may make about the news editor in the future. The news editor is skilled at managing the perceptions of the editor and succeeds with this stage of his plan. Subsequently, the political reporter is unable to convince the editor that he has been told a series of lies about her by the news editor. Thirdly, the news editor's attack is absolutely designed to undermine the political reporter's self-esteem, self-belief and self-confidence. He ignores her, treats her with contempt, grunts at her and remains resolutely punishing of her during the entire length of the campaign, all tactics which are designed to injure her inner self as she struggles to assimilate what is happening and react to it with her dignity intact.

Thirdly, does the news editor do these things in a deliberate attempt to remove personal power, reputational influence and/or organisational status from the political reporter and retain this power for himself? Absolutely, he wants to do all three of these things. His stated aim is to destroy the political reporter's career. Should he achieve this aim, he would negatively impact her personal power, reputational influence and organisational status. The news editor is a skilful adversary having honed his tactics during previous campaigns, each of which resulted in his female target leaving the newspaper. He makes life sufficiently uncomfortable for the political reporter so that she decides to resign, something which no doubt creates satisfaction on his part. However, he does not entirely succeed in his attempt to remove all three forms of power from her and retain that control for himself because the political reporter leaves very much on her own terms. She secures a favourable reference from him and, in doing that, she regains much of her personal power and reputational influence from him. She quickly finds employment elsewhere, and therefore re-establishes her organisational status. Her courageous and self-preserving decision to leave the newspaper protect her personal, reputational and organisational forms of power and influence, and enable her to build a new phase in her career albeit at a different publication.

Do the news editor's actions cause the team's energy to be diverted away from its work, and do they impact the team members' work and relationships subsequently? Yes, in very specific ways. Most members of the team remain passive when they witness bullying behaviour, preferring to keep their heads down and avoid drawing attention to themselves. This strategy is designed to minimise the risk that they might be targeted too. But it results in the team becoming a less sociable place to work, as each of them withdraws from their team colleagues and spends more time alone. Those who do support the political reporter, do so in a series of quiet asides out of the earshot of the news editor. We do not know how much time these two colleagues spend thinking about the bullying during working hours, but we can assume it does occupy their thoughts and take their energy away from their work as otherwise they wouldn't feel the need to talk with the political reporter about it. We can also say that the political reporter is left to cope with the significant distress of being bullied largely by herself. She mainly draws on her own personal resources which become thinly stretched as the campaign continues. Due to the news editor's refusal to send her any work assignments during the campaign, her excellent articles are lost to the newspaper and its readership.

Bullying Boss: Conclusions

What conclusions can we draw from this case study? Firstly, we can conclude that the resilience of the political reporter is sorely tested during the relentless campaign against her. Her personal resources are stretched to the limit as she copes with the daily assaults on her professionalism and personhood. The extent of the campaign is particularly difficult for the political reporter to cope with because it involves simultaneous attacks on her reputation, selfhood and livelihood orchestrated both behind her back and to her face, when she is alone and in front of her team colleagues. This is a mightily effective campaign created and sustained by a skilful team bully.

Secondly, we can conclude that lack of obvious, consistent, on-going support for the political reporter takes its toll on her. Although two of her colleagues do commiserate with her privately, offering some acknowledgement of her ordeal, no one in the team is prepared to stand up to the bully in the moment of an attack or subsequently. This degree of passive collusion results in the political reporter feeling isolated and alone as each of her colleagues witnessing an incident of bullying behaves as if nothing untoward has just happened.

Thirdly, we can say that the news editor's ability to manage the perceptions of the newspaper's editor makes his campaign against the political reporter all the more onerous for her to handle. As well as dealing with day-to-day bullying in the newsroom, she also contends with the fact that the editor has bought into a series of slanderous lies about her which the news editor has relayed to him. This adds greatly to the burden carried by the political reporter, because a would-be ally, one with significant organisational authority, is firmly of the opinion that she is failing at aspects of her job, and is so firmly of this opinion that he is not open to persuasion. The editor allows the news editor to manipulate his perceptions to such an extent that the political reporter is unable to convince him that what he has been told about her by the news editor consists of nothing but falsehood and slander.

Summary of Key Points from The Chapter

A healthy team is one in which you feel you belong and think you make a valued contribution. You and your team colleagues find ways to work together even though you might have divergent values, different ways of working and dissimilar outlooks on life. You make a point of behaving constructively when there is a disagreement to be resolved or a conflict about priorities or work goals. Your joint aim is to produce the best possible quality of work, and you all place this goal front and centre.

Team bullying involves at least one team colleague targeting you in a personal attack which is designed to undermine your inner self, undermine your ability to carry out your duties effectively, and/or undermine your reputation in the team. At the core of team bullying is the bully's desire to remove from you your personal power, your reputational influence and/or organisational status, and retain that control for themselves. A true team bully will make their relationship with you *about their power over you*, and will seek to injure your personhood, your credibility and/or your ability to carry out your duties.

Team bullying compromises the three contracts you have with your team: your work contract, your relational contact, and your psychological contract. It also changes the entire team dynamic. Even one incident of team bullying can take the energy of the team away from its work as you, and those team members who learn about or witness what happened, try to assimilate the experience. You and your team colleagues may react in different ways which could include becoming anxious, finding it difficult to concentrate, and needing to talk about what happened, actions which absorb the time and resources of the team, and take you away from your work.

True team bullying and aggressive but non-bullying behaviour are not the same thing. A team colleague who is poor at managing their emotion and lets their anger affect the way they deal with you needs to learn to handle themselves far better in the workplace. This team colleague may have a pressing need to learn emotional self-management skills and to take responsibility for dumping aggression at work. They may even push their relationship with you to breaking point, creating distress for you and other people in the team. But unless they intended to remove power from you and retain that control for themselves they are not responsible for an incident of team bullying.

A skilfully conducted campaign can have a devastating impact on your morale, health and well-being. If your colleagues choose to turn a blind eye to the bullying and do not actively support you, you can feel very alone and struggle to find the resources to cope. Your ordeal can be made more challenging when senior members of your organisation believe false information about you given to them by the bully as part of the campaign.

Questions for You to Consider

In this chapter, we have been examining what constitutes true team bullying as well as what the difference is between aggressive, non-bullying behaviour and true team bullying. You may now want to apply these distinctions to your own experience by responding to the following questions. You can jot down your answer to each in the space below it.

Call to mind an incident in which you were subject to aggression in your team.

1. What happened during the incident?

2. How did you react at the time? What impact did the incident have on you?

3. Assuming that one or more of your team colleagues witnessed the incident, how did they react at the time?

4. If no one witnessed it, whom did you tell? How did they react to what you said?

5. Looking back on it now, to what extent do you think that the incident was a personal attack on you?

6. Looking back on it now, to what extent do you think that the incident was designed to injure you personally or professionally, or to undermine your ability to carry out your duties?

7. Looking back on it now, to what extent do you think that the incident was about a desire on the part of your aggressive colleague to remove power from you and retain that control for themselves?

8. What impact did that incident have on your relationships with your wider team colleagues?

9. Looking back at what you have written, to what extent do you now regard what happened as an incident of true team bullying as opposed to an incident of aggressive, non-bullying behaviour?

Next Chapter

Chapter 2 will take you inside the mind of a team bully. It will explore how a team bully uses tactics which alter the balance of power in the team, retaining as much control as possible for themselves. The chapter will examine the methods a bully uses to subjugate a team, setting up dynamics which they hope will encourage colleagues to actively collude or passively enable their campaign. The chapter will also highlight the role that envy, jealousy and fear can play in the impetus to bully, and identify the key behaviours regularly employed by skilled team bullies.

Reference 1: Adapted from page 86 of *Free Yourself from Workplace Bullying* (Flourish, 2015).

Chapter 2
Inside the Mind of a Team Bully

A Team Bully is 100% Accountable 100% of the Time

In my coaching work and writing, I take the view that the responsibility for using bullying behaviour is 100% with the bully 100% of the time. I never blame the target – the person in your shoes – no matter what the context for the campaign. Different practitioners may take a different line to me, but the way I see it is that there are never any valid excuses for team bullying. There is a big difference between an effective team colleague and a team colleague who uses bullying behaviour. There is a big difference between an assertive, confident and effective manager, and a manager who gets their way by bullying. There is also a big difference between a manager who feels frustrated and worn-down by a team which consistently under-performs, and a manager who resorts to bullying to 'drive the team towards better performance'.

I also take the view that just about anyone can become a target in a campaign of team bullying – both confident and assertive individuals, and those who are meeker and struggle to use assertive behaviour. But whilst almost anyone could become a target, the truth is that people who struggle to assert themselves are more vulnerable to attack. Team bullies are on the lookout for signs of vulnerability and confusion, and when they find evidence of either, they seek to exploit it. Learning self-protective and self-preserving behaviour for use at the time of an attack is a priority for those of you who have a hard time using assertive behaviour.

However, while anyone in a team could be targeted, it is not true to say that anyone could decide to bully. Only those people who are prepared to handle their team interactions in a bullying way – only those who can square this approach with their conscience – will commence a campaign of team bullying. So, why would one member of a team decide to bully a colleague from their own team instead of working alongside that colleague in a spirit of co-operation, respect and goodwill?

Fear, Jealousy and Envy: Three Contexts for Team Bullying

Consider the following short examples:

- A member of a successful sales team in an advertising agency starts to doubt herself when one of her team colleagues wins a huge contract for the business. She begins to worry about her ability as a sales woman and becomes afraid that her managers will start to question her application and skills. Over a period of several weeks, despite the fact that there is no evidence to support her fears and no one in the management team has questioned her work, she begins to experience a strong fear of failure. Specifically, she fears the possibility of failing publicly and the humiliation she would feel when her team colleagues find out about her ruin. So, in a foolish and mistaken attempt to prevent a potential failure, she starts to target the team colleague who won the major contract. In a covert and stealthy campaign, she sabotages her colleague's reputation behind her back. In a series of subtly slanderous comments and remarks to the firm's senior managers she suggests that it was she, and not her colleague, who devised the successful sales strategy and that her colleague lacks both imagination and relationship-building skills. Over a period of weeks, she successfully persuades her managers that the true credit for the huge campaign is herself, and not her team colleague.

- Having been hired into a new role, an IT consultant quickly finds that he is out of his depth. He lacks the breadth of knowledge he needs to carry out his duties, and quickly experiences a dip in self-esteem and self-confidence. Rather than own up to the fact that he needs to find a role more suited to his skills, he becomes jealous of his team colleagues, each of whom is competent and capable, enjoys their job and likes working for the consultancy. He selects two of his team colleagues for a pernicious campaign of team bullying in which he seeks to deflect attention from his own genuine under-performance onto their supposed 'lack of application and effort'.

- A longstanding teacher in a primary school becomes frustrated at her stalled career progression. She observes younger members of her department being promoted more quickly than herself and becomes envious of their successes and increased incomes. Concerned that she is being left behind, she commences a campaign of team bullying to cut each of them down to size. Having been employed for many years in the school, she has well-established links with several of the senior teachers. She uses her informal influence with these colleagues to undermine the reputation and influence of her newly promoted rivals, and to suggest that she, rather than they, ought to be given greater responsibility. At the same time, she employs a combination of cutting comments, sarcasm and barely concealed contempt to unsettle her targets and place doubts in their own minds about their fitness for their new roles.

In each of these examples, the bully allows their *internally-generated fear, jealousy or envy to dominate their behaviour* and become the pretext for a campaign of team bullying. Instead of working to acquire the skills they need to be effective, or seeking clarification about what additional skills or attributes they need to develop, or confronting their own lack of suitability for a new role, each of the bullying characters makes a reprehensible choice, using their time, energy and attention to target a team colleague.

In my experience, jealousy and envy are often motivators behind a bully's instinct to commence a campaign. In the context of team bullying, I define jealousy as the desire to:

- Destroy the good that you have earned – your reputation, your personal qualities, your professional skills and/or your organisational status and rewards – *to prevent you from enjoying the benefits of them.*

- Drop the thought into the minds of team members that the bully could extend their campaign to include them too, and destroy the good that they have earned as well.

My definition of envy as it relates to team bullying is that the bully wants to:

- Take the good that you have earned – your reputation, personal qualities, professional skills and/or organisational status and rewards – *and acquire those things for themselves.*

- Drop the thought into the minds of team members that the bully could extend their campaign to include them too, and acquire the good they have earned as well.

There are many contexts for team bullying, each of which is unique to the bully involved. But I take the view that there is usually a combination of a factor *internal* to the bully in conjunction with a *situational* factor that together create the impetus to bully. In each of the examples above, the bully allows their internally generated fear, envy or jealousy to play out in a campaign of team bullying when, as they see it, a set of situational factors in the workplace go against them.

The Outcomes Team Bullies Want to Create

A team bully deliberately uses aggression at work. The aggression they employ could be active or passive in nature, but it is always used to intimidate, coerce, undermine and dominate. The exact nature of the bullying tools used will vary from bully to bully, depending on their intentions at the time and the dynamics they want to create. In employing these methods, team bullies want to achieve four things simultaneously. They want to:

- Remove as much power from you as possible, and transfer it to themselves.

- Limit the behavioural options accessible to you at the time of the attack.

- Create a bullying dynamic in their relationship with you – a dynamic which they want to establish as a clear pattern of behaviour between the two of you during the period of the campaign.

- Alter the team dynamic in such a way that established allegiances change, and team members who are not current targets defer to them or accept the bullying as 'normal' and fail to challenge it.

When the bully is successful, this combination of factors – removal of power, limiting behavioural choices, creating a bullying dynamic and frightening team members into submission – can leave you, the target, feeling powerless, anxious, unable to defend yourself and unsupported. When an attack occurs in front of team colleagues who outwardly appear unconcerned that you have just been assaulted it can be doubly disabling as you experience a debilitating degree of isolation at the very moment you most need support.

A skilled bully will vary the setting of their attacks. They could attack you in one-to-one encounters behind closed doors. They could attack your reputation behind your back when you are not in a position to defend yourself. They could attack you in front of some or all of your team colleagues to drop the thought into their minds that, should they cross the bully, they could receive similar treatment, deterring your colleagues from offering you support and leaving you feeling isolated and alone.

Consider the following list of some of the most common aims of a team bully. A team bully wants to:

- *Injure your self-esteem*: to cause you to doubt yourself and become confused about your self-worth.

- *Reduce your self-confidence*: so that you become increasingly unproductive.

- *Take direct actions which reduce the quality of your work*: to reduce your effectiveness in your role and injure your reputation in the eyes of your team colleagues.

- *Set you up to fail at key work assignments*: so that other people, including but not limited to your team colleagues, start to question your commitment or skills.

- *Exclude you from key team activities such as decision-making meetings, problem-solving discussions, information-giving forums or social occasions*: to isolate you from the team colleagues you work alongside.

- *Leave you feeling confused and on the back foot*: so that your belief in your own competence and ability to handle interactions with them and other team members is reduced.

- *Undermine your reputation professionally and personally*: to reduce your value in the eyes of your team members and yourself.

- *Reduce your influence in the team*: to undermine your ability to perform to your usual standard, and injure your credibility with team colleagues.

- *Scapegoat you for errors and mistakes you have not committed, some of which the bully may have been responsible for:* to call into question your value as a member of the team.

- *Discredit you in the eyes of your team members*: to undermine your relationship with them.

- *Make your team colleagues fearful that they might be targeted next:* to reduce the likelihood that these colleagues might stand up for you at the time of an attack or confront the bully after an attack.

The Skilled Team Bully's Toolkit

Every team bully has their own unique approach to bullying, preferring tactics and strategies which they experience as being most useful to them. Let's examine a range of the most common behaviours used by skilled team bullies. The following list is not designed to be exhaustive and you may be able to add to it behaviours you have observed.

Firstly, let's consider instances when the team bully attacks you in front of your team colleagues and /or during team meetings. They might:

- Exaggerate an error or oversight on your part so that they can characterise you as slipshod or lazy in front of your team colleagues. The bully may use a 'joking' tone to do this, dressing up the barb in a veneer of humour. A bully who repeatedly uses this tactic may be doing so because they recognise that doing a good job – and being recognised as a top performer in your team – is a key component of your self-esteem and one which they wish to undermine.

- Single you out for blame for mishandling a task or set of duties when it was they, not you, who messed up the work. In this case, the bully falsely accuses you in public and out of the blue, hoping that you will be so shocked that you will be unable to refute the allegation effectively.

- Fail to share important information with you to render you confused or at risk of appearing incompetent when these issues are discussed later with other members of the team.

- Make eye contact with everyone else in the team while persistently failing to make eye contact with you.

- Ignore or speak over your remarks to exclude you from the team dynamic, while making a point of responding verbally to everyone else who is present.

- Allocate you an unreasonable amount of work within a tight deadline so that, should you query the allocation, they can portray you as work-shy or lacking in commitment and application.

- Make a disparaging remark about you and immediately say something warm or compassionate to confuse you, making it more challenging for you to confront them.

Secondly, let's consider instances when the bully attacks you behind your back. The bully might:

- Regularly criticise your work to other people in the team in a series of subtle asides or more pointed comments. The misinformation the bully provides about you can take the form of outright lies, subtle slanders and fabrications or distorted half-truths.

- Completely misrepresent the quality of your work to team colleagues by claiming you have made errors and omissions which you have not made, perhaps adding that only their intervention prevented a catastrophe.

- Claim a recent piece of your work as largely their own, stating that without their assistance you would not have delivered on it on time or to standard.

- Take a fact about you (such as an important presentation you made to a senior member of the organisation) and distort it using a series of fabrications and slanders (such as the claim that the bully had to rescue you when you floundered part way through, or when you failed to answer a key question effectively). By basing the fabrications around a known fact – you really did give the presentation – the bully cleverly renders the lies more plausible.

- Arrange a team event, whether work-related or social, and subsequently fail to extend the invitation to include you. The bully does this to exclude you from team activities and leave you feeling isolated and left out.

- Arrange a team meeting for a specific time, but tell you that the meeting is actually starting a few minutes later. Prior to your arrival, the bully will present false information about your work or about you as a person to sway the mood of the meeting against you before you enter the room.

Thirdly, let's consider instances when the bully attacks you during one-to-one meetings when there are no witnesses. The bully might:

- Set you up to fail by arranging a briefing meeting to inform you about an upcoming piece of work you are to manage. The bully does outline your remit to you, but deliberately fails to tell you one or more key pieces of information which make your work impossible to complete on time and/or to standard.

- Start the meeting in a normal tone before suddenly employing direct and open aggression, sarcasm or scorn to undermine and intimidate you.

- Make a series of disparaging remarks to attack your professionalism, skills or behaviour, all of which consist of their *opinion* presented as a *series of facts.* Any attempt you make to refute these allegations will be met with equally emphatic justifications, also based on their opinions and value judgements rather than an objective commentary about your work or conduct

- Make a series of unfair and aggressive criticisms about your work or your behaviour. The aim is not to provide you with feedback to help you improve, but rather to undermine your self-confidence and self-belief.

- Introduce sudden physical aggression into their dealings with you to create menace. The bully might unexpectedly stand up, walk rapidly to where you are seated and stand over you to intimidate you. Or they might abruptly strike the table with the flat of their hand to drop the thought into your mind that they might strike you. Or they might pick an object up from the table, like a book or mug, and throw it across the room while making eye contact with you. Or they may actually throw a punch, striking your face or shoulders or another part of your body.

Let's explore how the themes of this chapter play out in a longer example.

Case Study 2: Rivalrous Peer

A kind and experienced nurse joins a busy day-care home run by the local social services department. She joins a team of twelve nurses who report to an on-site manager. The new nurse is pleased to get the job because it is near her home, and her shift patterns mean that she can start early and finish in time to collect her children from school. On her first day, one of her peers takes the time to welcome her to the day-care home and makes sure that they eat lunch together. During their lunch, the peer tells the new nurse that she is the longest-standing member of the workforce, has worked with the manager for a long time, and that her work is well-regarded. The new nurse is no fool and while not completely comfortable with the vibes she is getting from her peer, she decides that her new colleague is awkward socially and lacks confidence. Recognising that she is more able than her peer in social situations and quite confident, she responds openly to her new colleague and is completely unprepared for the turn of events which unfold over the next months.

From that afternoon onwards, her peer talks to her in a patronising voice, as if she is a child whom she wishes to admonish. The new nurse decides to confront her colleague late that afternoon, after the third instance of being subject to this distasteful behaviour. On hearing her new colleague's question about her tone of voice, the patronising peer tells her that she is 'being too sensitive' and that it's 'just a bit of banter'. Over the following week, the new nurse realises that her peer uses a patronising tone of voice to address her only when they are alone together. At all other times, the peer treats her with just enough warmth and good humour that the new nurse becomes confused and wonders if, indeed, she isn't being a bit too touchy.

During her first week, the new nurse makes a point of introducing herself to her other new team members, and finds them on the whole to be an open and supportive group of people. They are all busy with their work and, apart from lunchtimes and short breaks, rarely get a chance to talk about non-work issues. Nonetheless, the new nurse thinks she has formed good connections with several of her new colleagues and feels quietly pleased with her first week. She looks forward to working more closely with the team, but is disappointed to learn that her rota for the first month of her work regularly involves her working alongside her patronising peer.

Towards the end of the new nurse's second week, her peer starts to whisper about her new colleague behind her back. She suggests to the other staff at the day-care home that their new colleague is 'a bit soft', that she needs to 'get some experience', and that she needs to 'toughen up'. In front of the residents, the patronising peer refers to her new colleague as 'the newbie' and 'that one who's just joined', something she utters with a dismissive jerk of her head while rolling her eyes.

Whenever the two of them are working with a resident at the same time, the peer treats the new nurse to a combination of 'good-humoured banter' and blatant patronising. This blend of apparent warmth and veiled aggression leaves the new nurse on the back foot. She doesn't want to confront her colleague in front of a resident, but equally she doesn't want to let the incidents go without saying some-thing. After the third instance on the same day, she tells her peer that she needs a quick word with her. In the corridor outside the residents' rooms, she asks her peer why she needs to speak to her like that. The new nurse is shocked into silence as her peer tells her in smooth and commanding tones that 'none of the other staff can stand you either' and walks off. The new nurse is dismayed to hear a report that all her new colleagues dislike her and wracks her brains to understand what she could have done to engender such animosity. She walks into the staff kitchen and is surprised when the two nurses in the room, who had been giggling together as she walked in, notice her appearance and walk out without speaking to her.

On reflection, and despite the incident in the staff kitchen, the new nurse is not convinced that none of her colleagues likes her. She puts the incident in the kitchen down to the nurses being too busy to talk to her, and seeks out the three colleagues with whom she feels she has established the greatest liking and rapport. She approaches them one at a time, taking the calculated risk of quietly confiding some of her concerns to them. Their responses are similar: a shrug of the shoulders and comments to the effect that her peer has always been like that. One of these members of staff then takes a deep breath and tells the new nurse that their peer has always behaved that way, that she had been challenged about 'her snide side' before, but nothing had come of it and that is the way she is. As the new nurse assimilates this information, it further adds to her feeling that she may well need to toughen up and get on with things. Since everyone else puts up with it, she tells herself there is no reason she can't cope with it also. If she does challenge her peer further, she thinks she won't get any-where and nothing would be likely to change.

Over the next few weeks, the patronising peer escalates her campaign against the new nurse. The new nurse notices a series of neat hand-written annotations at the bottom of every page of the meticulous notes which she has made about each of the residents she is work-ing with. As she reads these handwritten observations, she realises that her peer has started to review everything she writes, making a series of completely different but not necessarily better proposals for managing the residents' health issues. The new nurse takes her work and the quality of her interactions with the residents in her care very seriously, and is taken aback that her peer would undermine her work so obviously and so consistently. She is disturbed that her peer would enter each resident's room after she has completed her duties, and write additional notes.

Then, while eating lunch with two of the other staff members, the patronising peer enters the lunch room and sits down. In a cold and cutting tone, she turns her head towards the new nurse and without making eye contact with her breathes the words 'you are making mistakes' at the new nurse. The new nurse feels bewildered and intimidated. Initially paralysed into silence, she daren't look at the other two nurses both of whom remain still and silent, looking down at their food. The new nurse summons all her strength, finishes her mouthful and turns towards the patronising peer. She asks her what she means, all the while acutely aware of the uncomfortable atmosphere in the room, the presence of her other two colleagues, and the fact that she is being undermined in public. The patronising peer tells her that she has organised a meeting with the day-care home's manager at which to 'review' the new nurse's work. The new nurse spirals into acute anxiety as she considers this information. She cannot understand how this meeting can be necessary and becomes very fearful.

Feeling friendless and uneasy at work, her sleep pattern alters and over the next few days the new nurse becomes constantly tired. She doesn't want to attend the 'review' meeting, doesn't know how to get out of it, and doesn't want to resign from a job she needs. As the date of the 'review meeting' approaches, she notices that she gets snappy with her children, and stops going to her yoga class.

Rivalrous Peer: Analysing the Team Dynamics

Let's examine the dynamics which play out between the rivalrous peer and the new nurse, and the dynamics at play within the wider nursing team at the day-care home.

From her earliest moments in the day-care home, the new nurse is subject to a campaign of team bullying by a peer whose behaviour she has no prior experience of. Although she is uncomfortable with her new peer's vibe during their initial time together, she doesn't recognise her behaviour for what it is: the initial stages of a campaign of team bullying. During lunch on her first day at work, the peer tells the new nurse that she is a long-standing member of the team, has worked closely with the manager for a long time and is appreciated for her work. But the new nurse's well-intentioned and kind demeanour result in her misinterpreting her new colleague's words. The new nurse is no fool, but she doesn't hear these boastful and self-serving comments as indicators of anything untoward. While not dismissing her discomfort, the new nurse doesn't hear them as malicious signs of envy and jealousy, and is unprepared for the skilful campaign orchestrated against her by the peer. The campaign consists of attacks to her face, behind her back, in the presence of her team colleagues and, eventually, and against her performance as well.

Why would the rivalrous peer act this way? The patronising peer is driven by a potent combination of envy and jealousy which result in her wanting to cut her more confident and socially skilled colleague down to size. From the moment she meets her, the patronising peer's latent envy and jealousy crystallise into hatred and she determines to bully. She has no reason to suppose that the new nurse is a threat to her, but she decides that she cannot allow someone more socially skilled than her to cramp her style. She wants to preserve her role as the most influential member of the nursing team, a role which provides her with prestige and kudos as the person closest to the manager. Neither of these desires – to eliminate the, as she sees it, 'opposition' and protect her status – will bring about what she really wants. That outcome – to be comfortable with herself – can only come from working to build her self-confidence, social skills and sense of self. Attacking a new member of the workforce *for possessing the very qualities she secretly wishes she could possess* will not bolster her flagging ego. Instead, it will take her mind off her work, it will injure her new colleague, and it will damage the care-home and its residents as the team dynamic becomes strained and work quality drops.

The rivalrous peer initially employs a mixture of veiled aggression in the form of patronising words and behaviour, coupled with suggestions to the new nurse that *she is the one who is at fault* for not being able to handle 'banter'. By switching the wrongdoing from herself to her target, the rivalrous peer wrong-foots her target and drops the thought into the new nurse's mind that it is *the new nurse* who is not tough enough and that *she* is quite within her rights to speak to her like that. While not totally convinced, the new nurse is thrown and does wonder if, in fact, she isn't taking things a bit too much to heart.

Having made her initial gambits, the patronising peer then steps up her campaign. She prepares the rota, making sure that the new nurse works regularly with her, giving her plenty of scope to bully when the two of them are alone. She extends her tactics to include speaking in derogatory tones about the new nurse to the residents, and to the other members of the nursing team. The patronising peer characterises the new nurse as lacking in experience and soft when she is actually knowledgeable, skilled and kind. The new nurse does not know that anything is being said about her. A more insecure character could have been derailed by the incident in the staff kitchen when two members of staff walk out of the room as she enters it, having just been giggling. The new nurse does not come to the conclusion that they are laughing at her, but decides that they have too much to do to speak with her. However, she is sufficiently nonplussed to seek out other members of staff and confide some of her concerns about her rivalrous colleague to them.

None of these colleagues has anything useful to tell her, beyond the fact that they all know the rivalrous peer 'is like that'. This is a pivotal moment for the new nurse. She knows that the peer is patronising and unpleasant to her. She now knows that other people have similar experiences of her unpleasantness, have confronted her in the past, and have not seen any subsequent behaviour change. The new nurse has a choice to make: put up with it and learn to live with it, or continue to confront the behaviours which she doesn't like, or both. She makes the first choice, telling herself that she doesn't have anything to gain from complaining about her peer to a manager who must know about her patronising demeanour and who, so far, has chosen to let the issues slide. But what the new nurse has not realised is that she is *subject to a campaign of team bullying.* She is only aware of her peer's patronising behaviour. She is unaware that this colleague also slanders her behind her back, undermines her reputation with the other nurses, and drops the thought into the minds of the residents that she is only so-so at her job.

It is only when the patronising peer starts to write handwritten notations at the bottom of the new nurse's notes, and then confronts her in front of two colleagues over lunch, that the new nurse understands that she is being set-up and personally targeted. Up until this point, the new nurse had assumed that her peer routinely uses a patronising voice. But, after discovering the handwritten notes and after the encounter over lunch, the new nurse realises that her peer's behaviour towards her is more calculating than routine condescension. She realises she is being targeted and her energy levels plummet.

She is now under no illusions about the size of the threat to her well-being and livelihood. She realises that the patronising peer has already spoken to the day-care home's manager about her, has already set up a meeting to 'review' her performance and has already concluded that she is 'making mistakes'. In the days leading up to the review meeting she cannot sleep and gets angry with her children.

Throughout all of these unsavoury developments, what role does the wider nursing team play in the evolving dynamics? The members of the wider nursing team are well aware of the tactics of the patronising peer. They have had to deal with them for a long time, and each of the nurses has come to their own accommodation with their colleague's bullying behaviour. While some of the nurses have complained in the past, none of these complaints has managed to alter their peer's behaviour, moderate her condescension or loosen the connection between her and the day-care home manager. Each member of the wider nursing team is also quite aware that the new nurse is the bully's latest target. But rather than stand up for her they *passively enable the new campaign of bullying.* They do this by failing to confront the slanderous comments the bully makes to them about the new nurse, and by failing to tell the new nurse that she is subject to a campaign of team bullying. Whether any of them believes what the patronising peer tells them about the new nurse – that she needs to 'toughen up' and 'get some experience' – remains to be seen. But their failure to warn the new nurse or offer her any support leaves the way clear for the patronising peer to pursue her campaign.

Rivalrous Peer: Conclusions

What conclusions can we draw from this scenario? We can say that, as a newcomer to the day-care home nursing team, the new nurse is at a severe disadvantage. She wants to make a good impression with her new colleagues and has no prior experience of the rivalrous peer from which to judge her demeanour or character. She is no fool, but she is understandably unprepared for the tactics employed against her.

We can also say that a combination of jealousy and envy motivates the rivalrous peer. Although persistently unpleasant to everyone in the day-care home, she hasn't felt the need to target anyone in a campaign of team bullying before. This time she moves from simply being patronising and aloof to using bullying behaviour in a carefully executed campaign. She targets someone who possesses the very qualities she would like to possess – kindness, social grace and confidence – safe in the knowledge that her long-standing alliance with the manager will stand her in good stead.

We can also say that the passive complicity of the existing workforce smooths the way for her. They all have personal experience of the challenge of tackling the patronising peer. They understand too well the tight bond between her and the manager. When they tiredly tell the new nurse that their peer is like that and that's all there is to it, they display the characteristics of people who feel powerless to alter a situation they find unpalatable. But they also *abrogate their responsibility to inform the new nurse about what she is up against*. They become part of the problem through their failure to confront a bully and their failure to support her target.

And what of the manager? When she agrees to hold the 'review' meeting, the manager actively enables the escalation of the campaign against the new nurse. She may or may not understand that the meeting is a vehicle for a set of bogus accusations against the new nurse. But she is quite aware of the character of the patronising peer, and has established and maintained close links with her. The manager's imprudent over-reliance on a member of staff who routinely demeans her colleagues calls her own integrity and judgement into question and, depending on the outcome of the 'review' meeting and the subsequent actions taken by the new nurse, may yet result in her having to confront her own irresponsibility and foolishness.

Summary of Key Points from the Chapter

A team bully is always responsible for their use of bullying behaviour, no matter what the circumstances. There is never any excuse for the use of bullying behaviour in a team, and there are no valid justifications for it. Team bullies are often motivated by a combination of fear, envy and jealousy. Instead of confronting themselves, working hard to ensure their success in their role, and developing the skills and attributes which make that success inevitable, they direct their energy, time and effort towards orchestrating a campaign of team bullying to undermine, scape-goat or eliminate the, as they see it, 'opposition'.

Team bullies want to remove power from you and retain it for themselves. They want to use behaviour which limits the choices available to you at the time of an attack, and which create a bully-ing dynamic between you. Importantly, they want to alter the team dynamic from active, trusting and open co-operation towards team members deferring to them, refusing to confront them, failing to support you, and regarding the bullying as 'normal' and not noteworthy.

Each bully has their own preferred bullying tactics. A skilled bully will attack you in one-to-one meetings when there are no wit-nesses, as well attacking you in front of other people and behind your back when you are not in a position to defend yourself. A skilled bully will simultaneously target your self-esteem and self-confidence, your reputation and credibility, your perform-ance and your relationships, often seeking to exclude you from team activities to isolate you when you most need to be included and supported.

Questions for You to Consider

In this chapter, we have been examining the mindset and tactics of a team bully. You may now want to apply this material to your own experience by responding to the following questions. You can jot down your answer to each in the space below it.

Call to mind a team colleague who you have observed using bullying behaviour, or who has bullied you.

1. What bullying tactics did you observe or experience your team colleague using?

2. In what situations did your team colleague choose to attack?

3. What do you think your bullying colleague was trying to achieve by acting this way?

4. To what extent do you think their bullying was motivated by fear?

5. To what extent do you think their bullying was motivated by jealousy?

6. To what extent do you think their bullying was motivated by envy?

7. What impact did the bullying have on the relationships in your wider team?

Next Chapter

Chapter 3 will explore the toxic impact of team bullying on the work and atmosphere in your team. It will outline how being targeted can result in plummeting self-esteem, toxic thoughts, and a level of isolation that can be debilitating. It will describe how team bullying alters established dynamics and allegiances within the team, unsettles and creates strain in relationships, and fosters tension between colleagues where none existed before. The chapter will also highlight how team bullying challenges everyone in the team to make a choice about whether to confront the bullying, remain passive in the face of the abuse, or actively collude with it.

Chapter 3
The Toxic Impact of Bullying
in a Team Environment

Personal Thresholds

Your personal threshold is unique to you. It is the point at which, if your personal level of resilience is breached by aggression, you are rendered vulnerable. Depending on the severity of the incident, you might feel disoriented, alarmed, afraid, anxious, confused or even go into shock. Everyone's personal threshold is specific and individual to them, so your personal threshold may be in a similar or dissimilar place to the thresholds of your team colleagues. Your personal threshold could be breached by one incident of team bullying which you experience as particularly damaging, or it may be breached by a number of incidents each of which is insufficient by itself to cause you to feel distress but which cumulatively do cause a breach in your resilience and result in you feeling punctured. Your personal threshold can be breached by non-bullying team aggression or team bullying, and each of you will have a different level of resilience. So, an act of aggression in your team which might not breach the personal threshold of a colleague could breach your personal threshold quite easily, and vice versa.

Many of my clients have a hard time with the concept of personal thresholds. They berate themselves for being 'weaker' than team colleagues who handle team bullying 'better' than they do. They point to the fact that a team colleague, subject to exactly the same bullying behaviour delivered in exactly the same way by the bully, was not injured by the experience; by contrast, they felt a potent mixture of fear, anxiety and powerlessness that has affected them ever since. In the tight-knit environment of a team which is subject to team bullying, comparisons like this can add greatly to the load carried by the target. Instead of placing responsibility where it rightly belongs – with the team bully – you are using vital energy beating yourself up about being insufficiently resilient. You may observe the team bully being equally combative and robust with other people who don't appear outwardly to be as adversely impacted as you are. But in coming to the conclusion that there is therefore something wrong with you, you are subtly but powerfully shifting the blame for your distress from the bully to yourself. You are blaming yourself for not being able to stand up to the bully. You are saying that you are at fault for being unable to cope. You are saying that is it *your fault that you are being successfully targeted.* These are deeply toxic thoughts because they do two things. Firstly, they place the responsibility for being targeted with *you* – the person subject to bullying behaviour – and make it *your fault* that you are being bullied in your team. Secondly, they result in you generating shame at being targeted and at feeling vulnerable, a combination of factors which means that you are beating yourself up for being, metaphorically, beaten up at work.

Those of you for whom this description resonates need to hear this: *you are not to blame for being targeted. You are not to blame* that your personal threshold has been breached and you have been hurt. In my philosophy, the only person responsible for wrongdoing in a scenario which includes bullying behaviour in a team environment is the person using those methods: the team bully. This means that bullying behaviour and non-bullying aggression are unacceptable and you do not have to tolerate them in your team. This is true regardless of whether the behaviour causes you significant distress or whether you are emotionally unaffected by it. Don't judge the degree of misconduct by your emotional reaction to it. Bullying behaviour and non-bullying aggression are what they are: wrong and unacceptable.

Resilience is a different issue. Your level of resilience governs the degree to which you feel distressed by bullying behaviour or non-bullying aggression. Reading this book will enable you to *learn greater resilience skills,* to acquire a wider range of effective self-protective and self-preserving behaviours, and to develop a repertoire of tactics which will enable you to make clear choices at the time of an attack, protecting your inner self from assault. These developments will equip you with a greater capacity to withstand team bullying. They will provide you with clarity about how to put the issues back to the bully at the time of any future attack, and enable you to remove yourself from future incidents without feeling distressed and overwhelmed. The starting point for all these fruitful developments is to cease castigating yourself for being targeted by a team bully, and instead use that energy to learn to combat bullying behaviour simply and straightforwardly. Resilience, like self-confidence, is a learned skill. And it is a skill you can learn given commitment and time.

Let's now consider the possibility that, should your personal threshold be sufficiently breached by experiences of team bullying, you may experience some degree of trauma.

Trauma and Overwhelm: Two Outcomes of Team Bullying

Trauma is overwhelming emotional reactions that are too intense to be processed using the coping strategies you normally employ in your day-to-day life. If you are upset, you are likely have a series of tried and tested coping strategies that enable you to return to equilibrium such as talking about what happened to you with someone you trust, going for a walk in the countryside or a park, spending time with your pets, playing sport or spending time with family members. There are potentially hundreds of alternative options available to you and you will rotate between them, and try out new ones, during the course of normal life events.

Traumatic experiences take you over your personal threshold making it difficult to process the emotion and therefore *leave the experience behind.* Your system cannot contain the intensity of the emotion, and your usual coping strategies don't enable you to re-establish equilibrium. The experience remains unprocessed and alive in your psyche, sapping your energy. It can contribute to you starting to make a series of changes to the way you think and behave, and to what you believe. There are many ways in which traumatic overwhelm can affect your life. Some of the changes you make may be unconsciously derived, and you may not even be aware of them until someone points them out to you. In each instance, the change you make is your way of adapting to the *presence of trauma in your life.* You may start to:

- *Behave differently:* you might spend less time with team colleagues during coffee and lunch breaks, stop participating in your favourite hobbies and pastimes, start to drink more alcohol, start to isolate yourself and meet less often or not at all with your friends and family.

- *Think differently about yourself and other people:* you might start to value yourself less highly than you did before the bullying, regard yourself as less able at your job than you normally would, or arrive at the conclusion that certain people in your life are not actually as close to you as you thought they were.

- *Generate beliefs about yourself which are not factual or true but which seem true to you:* you might start to believe that no one actually cares that you are being abused in your team, that your true nature is to be submissive and there is nothing you can do about it, or that fighting back is pointless and will only make matters worse.

De-toxification from the trauma of team bullying is a personal, individual journey and each of you will tread a different path on that journey. Trauma *can* be processed safely and effectively so that it doesn't affect your day-to-day life anymore. This is true even for those of you who are struggling with severe trauma, and can't quite believe that assurance at the moment.

Plummeting Self-Esteem, Shattered Confidence, Toxic Thoughts

By its very nature, a campaign of team bullying is designed to injure either your self-esteem or self-confidence (your inner self); or your reputation (your workplace connections and relationships); or your ability to carry out your work (your livelihood). The challenge for you, as a person subject to team bullying, is how to function effectively when you are at work and under attack. And that challenge can be considerable. Let's consider some more of the specific changes in your day-to-day life which you might experience should you be subject to a full-on campaign orchestrated by a skilled team bully.

1. *Your self-esteem could lower as you start to think less of yourself:* you may regard yourself as less able, less competent or less worthwhile a person than before you were targeted. Your self-image may suffer as you start to generate toxic, self-critical thoughts about yourself. The toxic thoughts you generate further undermine you by going around and around your head even when the bully isn't present or is present but isn't bullying you. In this case, your toxic

self-talk effectively continues the team bully's work for them as you criticize yourself in the quiet of your own mind, taking your energy away from the task of protecting yourself from another attack, and away from your work.

2. *You may lose confidence in yourself:* this may be because you don't know how to defend yourself at the time of an attack, don't know how to prevent a future attack or because you feel permanently vulnerable while you are at work. One of the consequences of finding yourself in this mire can be that you no longer trust your judgement or instincts, and quickly begin to doubt yourself even in situations where you used to be spontaneous and comfortable. This can be true even if you were a self-confident and buoyant character before the campaign began.

3. *You may feel anxiety and self-doubt as you worry about when the next attack might take place:* the anxiety could take the form of mild apprehension and uneasiness about going to work, going to team meetings or having an encounter with the team bully. But it could also take the form of full-on dread that results in debilitating levels of anxiety, vomiting, cold clammy sweats and sleepless nights. Should the team bully employ the strategy of being intermittently 'nice' to you rather than consistently bullying you, your anxiety and self-doubt could be greater due to your confusion about when the next unpredictable attack might occur. You may understandably ask yourself the question: 'Is it me? The team bully was nice to me last time I met them so perhaps it's *me* misjudging them.'

4. *You may feel angry:* you may not be able to express your anger with the bully either because it is overwhelming and potentially explosive or because you don't want to behave in ways which seem similar in your mind to the bully's behaviour. Alternatively, you may feel angrier with passive bystanders in the team who carry on as if nothing untoward is happening whilst witnessing you being abused. You may also become uncharacteristically angry at home or with friends, and you may find that your fuse is much shorter than usual at work or that you become irritable much more easily.

5. *You may find that you have less get-up-and-go than usual:* it is likely that much of your energy will go inwards to help you cope with the

assaults you are experiencing. Less of your energy will be available to enable you to interact with team colleagues and other people, or to attend to your work duties. You might feel constantly tired, lacking drive and motivation or you may lack your usual levels of enthusiasm for your work. These factors could compromise your ability to perform to your usual standard, leaving you open to accusations of under-performance which a bully may incorporate into their campaign.

6. *You may be unable to speak about what has happened to you at all or in sufficient detail to convey the severity of what you are experiencing:* depending on the extent of the bullying, you may be unable to speak about what has happened to you at all or unable to share sufficient detail with your colleagues or confidantes to create a compelling narrative. This doesn't mean that your protest is bogus, more that you need to de-toxify so that you can process what has happened to you and make sense of it enough to be able to speak about it safely.

7. *You may experience a range of debilitating physical symptoms:* these could include feeling nauseous before going into work, developing headaches or migraines, experiencing palpitations, having recurrent or permanent back ache, developing skin conditions, experiencing sweating or shaking, losing your appetite or eating more than usual. You may also get repeated infections or viruses as your system struggles to cope with the assaults and your level of immunity lowers. You may experience disturbed sleep.

8. *You may feel isolated and alone*: your feelings of hurt can be especially acute if one or more of your team colleagues know that you are being bullied but doesn't offer you support at the time of an attack or afterwards. In cases where you enjoyed a close connection with them before the campaign, your colleagues' inertia can add greatly to your levels of trauma and confusion.

All of these burdens add to the strain you are under from team bullying, and for some of you, make it imperative that you learn self-protective and self-preserving skills so that you know how to protect yourself at the time of any future attack, and ensure that you are not successfully targeted in the future.

Altered Allegiances, Strained Relationships: The Impact of Bullying on the Team Dynamic

We have been discussing how your experience of being targeted by a team bully can result in a dramatic loss of self-esteem and self-confidence. We have also touched on how you can feel very alone in a team where your trusted colleagues turn a blind eye to the bullying. Let's explore this latter issue in more detail.

The following diagram illustrates the double-whammy of being subject to bullying behaviour in front of your team colleagues whilst also coping with the shocking realisation that your none of your team colleagues is prepared to acknowledge the incident, speak out against it or offer you active support. Patterns of passive enabling by team colleagues who witness an attack play straight into the hands of the person targeting you. Consider the following diagram which I have adapted from page 71 of *Free Yourself from Workplace Bullying: Become Bully-Proof and Regain Control of Your Life* (Flourish 2015). The diagram starts with the circle at twelve o'clock.

Diagram 1: How Team Bullying Impacts You and Alters Team Dynamics

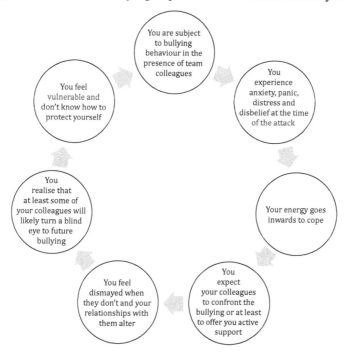

Let's now examine how these themes play out in greater detail.

Case Study 3: Isolated

A busy hotel kitchen employs twelve people who produce excellent food for a variety of regular customers. The team comprises a head chef, assistant chef and pastry chef, as well as a sous chef and eight kitchen workers. Although the hotel experiences occasional turnover of kitchen staff, the team is a stable, happy and friendly place, albeit the staff do grumble about having to work so frantically at peak times of the day. One of the newer members of staff is the talented assistant chef who quickly establishes liking and respect with his colleagues in the kitchen, each of whom appreciates his warmth and good humour.

Three months into his employment, the assistant chef becomes subject to a campaign of team bullying by the head chef. The attacks take place during the busiest periods in the kitchen, at lunchtime and dinnertime when all the team members are present but rushed off their feet preparing meals. The head chef's tactic is to sidle up behind the assistant chef when he is engrossed in his work, and employ a potent combination of caustic comments, sarcasm and downright rudeness to repeatedly question his competence, skill and application. Initially stung by the unwarranted criticism, the assistant chef soon becomes demoralised as he realises that none of his colleagues is willing to acknowledge that he is being targeted.

At the time of the attacks, the sous chef and the pastry chef, along with the other kitchen staff and the waiters who are present at the time, all turn a blind eye, busying themselves collecting or delivering orders or suddenly remembering an ingredient or condiment they need which is stored on the other side of the large kitchen. Subsequent to each attack, no one makes eye contact with the assistant chef, consoles him or speaks to him. He feels isolated and alone, and worries that he is being ostracised at the time when he most needs both the support of his colleagues and to feel part of the team.

As the campaign continues, the sous chef starts to dread that she may become a target even though there is no evidence that the head chef intends to start a campaign against her. Terrified of the prospect of being singled out for castigating comments, she starts to ingratiate herself to the head chef. She makes a point of speaking to him each time she sees him, and then begins to tell him snippets of gossip about the assistant chef. Initially, she confines herself to telling the head chef truthful information only. She mentions to the head chef that the assistant chef has recently split from his partner and that he does not like the place where he is living. But then she starts to fabricate a series of lies about the assistant chef including the false-hood that he regularly takes the remains of the crème caramel and other desserts home with him, and frequently pilfers small amounts from the communal tips which the waiters collect.

The other members of the kitchen recognise that the sous chef and head chef seem to be spending quite a bit of time together. They surmise that the sous chef has started to collude with the head chef, and the atmosphere in the kitchen becomes sullen and wary. The assistant chef remains isolated and alone, subject to constant belittling comments and unjust criticisms from the head chef. The other members of the kitchen staff keep themselves to themselves, each concentrating on their individual tasks, and have as little to do with him or one another as possible. Two weeks after the sous chef starts to collude with the head chef, and four weeks after the campaign commenced, two members of the kitchen team hand in their resignations and another member of the team starts to look for alternative employment. One long-standing customer complains about the quality of his tarte pommes, and another tells the waiter that his food lacks its usual tastiness. The restaurant experiences a drop in its income for the first time ever as long-standing customers elect to eat elsewhere.

Isolated: Analysing the Team Dynamics

Let's examine the dynamics which play out among the members of the kitchen team. In this example, a head chef starts to bully an outgoing and popular assistant chef in full view of everyone else in the kitchen. During these attacks, which take place during the busiest times of the working day when the assistant chef has the most work to do, none of the other kitchen staff acknowledges the bullying behaviour. They each continue working on their individual tasks and do not offer the assistant chef any support at the time of an attack or afterwards. The assistant chef quickly feels isolated and alone, abandoned by the very people he used to enjoy friendly workplace interactions with. He is dismayed to realise that while he was popular and liked before he was subject to team bullying, none of his erstwhile friends is willing to support him or offer him life-giving connection during the campaign.

But then things take a turn for the worse. The sous chef decides that she cannot take the risk that the head chef might decide to bully her. At the time she makes this decision, there is no evidence that the head chef intends to bully her. He reserves his castigating comments and belittling jibes for the assistant chef only. Nonetheless, terrified that she may also be targeted, the sous chef decides to collude with the head chef in the hope that becoming his 'ally' might preclude him from targeting her. She cannot know for sure whether her tactics of collusion really will protect her or not but, driven by her fear and disregarding the other consequences of her behaviour, she is prepared to give this tactic a try in the hope that it will work for her.

Our sympathy is entirely with the assistant chef as he finds himself in the unfortunate situation in which every single member of the team he works in either turns a blind eye and passively enables the bullying, or actively colludes with the bully to facilitate the bullying. Every one of them ignores his plight and puts their own interests first, in a series of self-serving decisions. What could account for their behaviour?

As soon as the campaign against the assistant chef commences, every other member of the kitchen staff – including the waiters who observe what is happening when they go into the kitchen – has a choice to make. They are no longer members of a friendly, open and safe kitchen team but are now part of a team in which one member of that team, the head chef, is bullying another member of that team, the assistant chef. Their experience of their workplace undergoes a subtle but powerful alteration. As soon as the team members recognise that the assistant chef is subject to bullying behaviour, and that that behaviour is being employed by the head chef in full view of all of them, every team member must decide how they will react. Do they:

- *Stand up to the bullying head chef:* by confronting the bullying, and offering active support to the assistant chef either at the time of an attack or shortly afterwards?

- *Adopt the position of passive enabler:* by carrying on with their duties as if nothing abusive is happening, and allowing the bullying to continue without saying or doing anything about it, either at the time or afterwards?

- *Actively collude with the head chef:* by contributing to and promoting the on-going campaign?

Sadly for the assistant chef, each member of the kitchen staff chooses to do either the second or the third of these three things. At the time of each attack, the pastry chef, the kitchen workers and the waiters all busy themselves with their individual tasks, refusing to acknowledge or confront the acts of bullying towards the assistant chef. Some of them do this because they are more comfortable deferring to the head chef, who they regard as their manager, than confronting him. Others do so for more complicated reasons. Their failure to take a positive stand and support the assistant chef is so complete that they don't even make eye contact with him or offer him a quiet word of encouragement after an assault. They leave him completely alone while he deals with a relentless level of unjust criticism from the head chef. Each of them does this because they don't want to get involved. They take the view that the bullying is something that is occurring between the head chef and the assistant chef, and that it doesn't concern them. They think that to get involved is to potentially make trouble for themselves down the line, so they effectively ignore the bullying and carry on with their work.

The sous chef takes a different stance. Her active participation in the campaign, albeit as a colluder rather than the instigator of the bullying, enables the head chef to strike at the assistant chef with greater potency. The sous chef is a duplicitous figure. At once scared of being targeted and also venal in nature, she decides to 'protect' herself from possible future assault by working with the head chef to facilitate his attacks on his target. The information she provides him with is initially about areas of vulnerability in the life of the assistant chef: that he has recently split from his partner and that he doesn't like where he is living. To a skilled bully like the head chef, these are enticing pieces of information as they enable him to make his personal attacks on the assistant chef that bit more precisely targeted. But not satisfied with 'protecting' herself by giving personal details about the assistant chef to the head chef, the sous chef then starts to lie about the assistant chef. She fabricates untruths about him in a series of slanders which she delivers to a bully she expects will seize on them and use in his campaign. She does this to ingratiate herself with the head chef, and the tactic she employs is to feed the head chef's enmity for the assistant chef in a series of slanderous falsehoods. The sous chef tells the head chef that his target steals food from the kitchen and money from the waiters' tips, information which the bullying head chef could use in a number of ways. He could incorporate these defamatory accusations into his campaign in the form of specific verbal assaults or he could mention them to the hotel's managers to injure the reputation of the assistant chef. Or he could do both of these things.

As soon as the campaign commences, each member of the kitchen team has a clear moral choice to make and, in this example, none of them comes out of the scenario with their integrity intact. Each of them allows their fear or their personal inertia or their lack of integrity to dominate their actions, and thereby enable a vicious campaign of team bullying. The fallacy of their position is the idea that by turning a blind eye *there will be no unpleasant personal consequences for them to deal with.* This is not true. As the campaign continues, and the relationships of the kitchen team members become compromised, so the quality of the food produced in the kitchen deteriorates and customers start to complain. Then they start to eat elsewhere and the restaurant's takings decrease. Now there are consequences for all of them to face as the clientele of the restaurant vote with their feet and the livelihoods of at least some of the kitchen staff are put in jeopardy.

Isolated: Conclusions

What conclusions can we draw from this scenario? Firstly, we can say that the assistant chef is very unlucky indeed that the entire kitchen staff either turns a blind eye or, in the case of the sous chef, actively colludes with the bully. This unfortunate situation results in him feeling alone and isolated at the time of each attack and afterwards. His choices are limited. He can stay and be bullied, hoping to get through it as best he can. Or he can leave and seek employment elsewhere. He chooses the former option, and tries his best to brace himself against subsequent attacks.

Secondly, we can conclude that the sous chef is a duplicitous and complex character. At once terrified of being targeted herself, she is also quite willing to add to the misery of the popular and likeable assistant chef by actively colluding with the head chef against him. Her decision to do this is motivated by fear and anxiety. She is genuinely afraid that she might be targeted next, even though there is no evidence in the head chef's behaviour that he is about to target her. Permanently on tenterhooks, she does not know when, or if, a campaign against her might commence. A combination of her inner tension coupled with the presence of a skilled bully leading the team, results in her making the unwise decision to collude. This decision is unwise for two reasons. Firstly, everyone else in the team now knows her true nature. Any goodwill which her colleagues had been willing to extend to her will no longer be on offer. In a small team, the diminution of her colleagues' respect and openness towards her will affect her day-to-day experience in myriad ways. Secondly, her actions do not at all preclude the head chef from targeting her. Rather, they reveal to him that she is a venal character, someone who is not to be trusted and someone whose 'support' of his campaign is primarily about her own fragility.

Thirdly, we can say that the restaurant owners need to demonstrate much better management of the kitchen. By allowing the head chef to bully his assistant chef, frighten the rest of the staff into silence and inaction, and do so for months on end, they demonstrate a shocking lack of concern for the welfare of their staff and the future of their business. It is a fallacy for business owners to think that customers are not ultimately impacted by team bullying. In the kitchen, morale dips, relationships become strained and the quality of the food lowers. Staff feel anxious, they make mistakes and the speed and quality of service slows down. Some customers complain. Some leave and start to eat elsewhere. Eventually, staff leave too. By failing to take sufficient interest in their business and allowing a bully free reign to operate in their kitchen, the managers of the restaurant are taking a big risk with their income and their business's reputation.

Summary of Key Points from the Chapter

Your personal threshold is the point at which you become vulnerable should you be subject to bullying behaviour. Your personal threshold is unique to you, which means that the way you experience an incident of team bullying – whether you are the target or a witness – may be quite different from the way another member of the team experiences the same instance. An incident which renders you vulnerable could be shrugged off by one of your team colleague's as less damaging or not damaging at all. This does not imply that you are 'weak'. Rather, it implies that your personal threshold has been breached but your colleague's personal threshold has not been breached. Learning self-protective and self-preserving skills is vital for those of you with a lower personal threshold.

It is important that you don't beat yourself up should your personal threshold be breached. The offence does not lie with you, it lies with the colleague who uses bullying behaviour, something which is unacceptable in a team. In my philosophy, a team bully is always 100% responsible for their behaviour 100% of the time. No excuses.

When your personal threshold is breached, you can experience a range of emotional reactions from mild apprehension through to full-on dread. You may even become traumatised. Trauma is overwhelming emotional reactions that are too intense to be processed using the coping strategies you would normally employ in your day-to-day life. Should you become traumatised, you may find that your behaviour, thoughts and feelings alter.

As a result of being bullied, you may experience plummeting self-esteem and lowered self-confidence as you start to conclude that you are not as worthwhile a person as you thought you were. You may feel isolated, even abandoned, if your team colleagues do not actively support you at the time of an attack, or shortly afterwards. Colleagues who don't support you are passively enabling the bullying via their inaction. They may do this out of a fear of being targeted next or because of a level of apathy or disinterest in the campaign. If the bully is their manager, team colleagues may also adopt the role of passive enabler out of a misguided belief that they ought to defer to authority.

Some of your colleagues, albeit a minority, may actively collude with the bully in which case they will take steps to facilitate the campaign against you. They may do this out of the misguided belief that working with the bully will make it less likely that they will also be targeted. This is not actually true, as the bully could target them too should they wish to.

Any team in which one member subjects another to bullying behaviour will experience strained relationships and altered allegiances as a direct consequence of the campaign. It is a fallacy for managers to believe that taking the easy path and not confronting the bully will serve their business well. The most punishing personal impact of a campaign is always on the target and it can be devastating. But team bullying also affects the entire team dynamic. Managers and business owners who take the easy option by failing to confront bullying set themselves up for a range of consequences which they won't be able to ignore. These include reduced work quality, resignations, falling sales and lowered income as the team's work performance declines and the morale of the team members dips.

Questions for You to Consider

In this chapter, we have been examining the impact of team bullying on your personal well-being and on your relationships with your team colleagues. You may now want to apply this material to your own experience by responding to the following questions. You can jot down your answer to each in the space below it.

Call to mind an incident in which you were subject to team bullying. The incident could be a one-off example of bullying behaviour or a campaign against you.

1. What happened during the incident?

2. Looking back on the incident now, what impact did it have on your personal well-being immediately afterwards and in the following days or weeks?

3. Looking back on it now, in what ways did your behaviour and your thoughts alter as a result of being subject to the bullying?

4. Which of your team members was present at the time of the incident, or heard about it shortly afterwards?

5. To what extent did these colleagues offer you support during the attack or shortly afterwards? What form did their support take?

6. What impact did receiving the support of your colleagues have on your well-being?

7. To what extent did any of your colleagues passively enable the bullying? What did they say or do which leads you to this conclusion?

8. To what extent did any of your colleagues actively collude with the bullying? What did they say or do which leads you to this conclusion?

9. Looking back at what you have written, in what ways did your experience of your team alter as a result of the bullying and your colleagues' reactions to it?

Next Chapter

Chapter 4 will explore how a team bully grooms their targets prior to commencing a campaign. It explores what team grooming is, what it feels like to be groomed in front of your team colleagues, and why it can be so confusing. The chapter highlights a range of well-intentioned but ineffective strategies for handling team grooming at the time it occurs, as well as a range of influential responses which will protect you at the time of an incident.

What You Will get From Chapters 4 to 9

The preceding chapters of this book have described what team bullying is, why a team bully might want to bully, how bullying alters team dynamics and how it can impact your health and well-being. From Chapter 4 onwards, we will be exploring effective strategies to use to combat grooming and bullying in your team. These strategies take the form of simple but powerful behavioural techniques which simultaneously protect you and combat the bullying by altering the bullying dynamic in your favour at the time of the attack. Chapter 4 will focus on effective strategies to use to protect yourself during an incident of team grooming, an event which occurs during the period *before a campaign commences.* Chapters 5-8 focus on how to protect yourself during incidents of team bullying which occur *within the course of a campaign.* Chapter 9 focuses on how to regain your self-confidence and self-belief *whether the campaign is on-going or after it has ceased.*

I take the view that most powerful and influential moment to respond to grooming or bullying behaviour is *at the time of the attack,* not afterwards. The moment of attack is the optimal opportunity to alter or prevent the bullying dynamic from becoming an established part of the interactions between you and the team bully. Strange though it may sound, it is in these moments that a true team bully – when handled in a carefully crafted way by a target who knows how to defend themselves – is most likely to think twice about repeating their grooming or bullying behaviour with you.

It is never too late to start to confront a bully in this way. The campaign against you could be established or it could be in its infancy. Either way, the principles illustrated in the rest of this book will be effective in enabling you to alter the team bullying dynamic in your favour during the next attack. Should the campaign against you be well advanced, there is no need to look back and regret that you didn't know how to defend yourself during earlier incidents. Don't get sidetracked and dwell on lost opportunities. Instead, confront during the next incident and alter the power dynamics in your favour then and there. An established bully will be all the more defeated because they won't be expecting you to confront them effectively, and will likely be deeply into a false sense of their own 'power over you' from previous uncontested incidents. A well-judged confrontation by you now may well floor them.

All of the techniques which we discuss in chapters 4 to 8 centre on you, the target, becoming more able at:

- Putting the issues back to the would-be bully.

- Laying down a boundary at the time of an attack.

- Sending back a clear message to them that you see what they are doing, know how to defend yourself, and will not be a straight-forward person to target.

This is possible, even for those of you who don't believe it yet or who have a hard time using assertive behaviour.

However, let's be clear that this is a complex area, one that requires empathy and compassion. Those of you who have been severely bullied in your team may be overwhelmed by your experiences. You may experience trauma, distress and a degree of powerlessness. Your performance may drop as your energy goes inwards to cope with the grooming and bullying you are subject to, and the strain these inci-dents place on your team relationships. Currently, you may not know how to protect yourself in the event of further attack and, depend-ing on how long you have been targeted in your team, you may feel abandoned and unsupported by your team colleagues and other people in the organisation who know that bullying is happening, and who don't take effective measures to prevent it. You may even be angrier with the leaders of your organisation who know what is happening and aren't doing anything about it than you are with the team bully themselves.

By digesting the learning from the rest of this book, you will acquire the knowledge, insight and skills you need to enable you to respond to team grooming and bullying in the moment, so that you can leave those encounters without feeling overwhelmed, confused and dis-tressed, and avoid feeling the potentially paralysing levels of anxiety that accompany the prospect of another encounter with the bully.

Chapter 4
Grooming in Your Team

What is Team Grooming?

Those of you with personal experience of being targeted by a team bully may be able to look back on what happened and identify a specific moment when the bully first struck. It might have been an incident which occurred in front of some or all of your team colleagues. Or it might have been an incident in a meeting between you and the team bully behind closed doors. Either way, there was a specific moment in your relationship when the bully started to do things differently. In that moment, the bully changed their relationship with you from one in which two colleagues were collaborating to get tasks completed into one in which they decided to remove power from you in a personal attack which you experienced as punishing and undermining. You may not have been expecting the bully to use aggression to throw you off guard, or to attack you out of the blue. You may have felt vulnerable, confused or uncertain about what had happened, and why it happened. And in that split second of confusion, you may have been unable to find something to say which protected you and sent back a message to the bully not to behave that way towards you again.

But, if you look further back, beyond the first incidents in the campaign, you may also be able to identify one or more incidents that were not clear-cut incidents of bullying, but which were confusing and troubling nonetheless. Perhaps you felt tense after an encounter with the colleague who eventually bullied you. Or maybe you felt self-doubt as you struggled to assimilate a particular incident involving that colleague. Looking back on it now, you may not have understood what was happening in those moments. You registered that something was wrong, that something untoward had happened, but you couldn't put your finger on what it was, why it was significant or what to do about it. What was happening is that you were being *groomed* by the team bully to see how susceptible you might be to a subsequent campaign of team bullying. The confusing behaviour is them saying to you: 'If you put up with that, I'm likely to escalate.'

Grooming occurs before a campaign of team bullying commences. It is the team bully's way of making an assessment about whether you will be a suitable target for a campaign, and what situations will be most conducive for them to attack you. Some team bullies use a number of grooming interactions to make their assessments. Others may employ just one incident and then move swiftly to a campaign of team bullying. An incident of grooming could be conducted in a one-to-one encounter with you or in the full view of some or all of your team colleagues. A bully who grooms you in a one-to-one meeting is testing how vulnerable *you* are. A bully who grooms you in full view of other team colleagues *is* testing how vulnerable you are but is also testing how *everyone else in the team handles the grooming behaviour*. In each incident of grooming, the bully deliberately uses behaviour which tests the waters to see how you, and any colleagues present at the time, respond to their veiled or overt aggression. They carefully observe what you and your colleagues say and do, and make an assessment about whether you will be someone with whom they will find it straightforward to create a bullying dynamic. In each incident of grooming in front of the entire team, the bully deliberately uses behaviour which tests the waters to see how the *team members* respond, enabling them to carefully observe the responses of those witnessing the incident and make an assessment about whether these team members will actively oppose them, actively support you, or remain passive, silent and still, should they move into a campaign against you.

It is important that you recognise an incident of grooming for what it is, either at the time it occurs or soon afterwards. That way you can mentally prepare for your next encounter with the would-be bully, arm yourself with self-protective behaviour, and be on your guard for repeat instances in the following days and weeks. The rest of this chapter will show you how to do that effectively.

Handling Team Grooming Effectively: Mitigating Distress and Toxic Feelings

At its heart, bullying is about power. What an incident of grooming achieves for the would-be bully is to give them an opportunity to observe how you might react to bullying behaviour: in other words, how well equipped you are with self-preserving strategies that enable you to retain your power, and retain control, under pressure.

If you react with vulnerability or confusion, the would-be bully may well be encouraged to try again, either with a subsequent act of grooming or by going straight to a campaign of team bullying. However, if you react with firm or even robust boundaries and a clear message that says 'don't try that with me' some would-be bullies will think twice. Many will desist entirely. Others may try again, just to see how determined and resilient you are. Why will many desist? Because, in my experience, most bullies only use the room for manoeuvre that targets inadvertently give them. In other words, by learning what behaviours to avoid, and by learning what to say and do in the moment of being groomed, you can learn to retain your power under pressure. This is a crucial self-protective strategy with which to combat team grooming and bullying.

The key learned skill which will enable you to resist bullying behaviour is that of *retaining your power under pressure*. If you can retain some or all self-control in a grooming encounter or, indeed, during an actual campaign of team bullying, you can leave each incident without feeling overwhelmed, abused and distressed. For many of the people I have spoken to and worked with over the past twenty-five years, it is the feelings of overwhelm, distress and abuse that are so toxic for them, along with the knowledge that they did not know how to protect themselves at the time of an attack. This debilitating combination of factors play on their mind, causing them to use precious energy beating themselves up about *what they failed to do at the time* rather than using their energy to learn how to combat grooming and bullying effectively. This results in them feeling vulnerable and ill-prepared for the next attack, further impairing their already fragile self-esteem, self-confidence and self-belief.

Key Factors in Handling Team Grooming Effectively

Knowing what to say and do at the time of an incident of team grooming – or of team bullying – is a key learned skill for those of you concerned that you may be vulnerable to future attack. It is the *act of making a choice at the time of an attack* – in other words, retaining for yourself the right to decide what you will do, what you will say and how you will behave – that mitigates the toxic overwhelm and feelings of being abused that otherwise are so difficult to process after the event, and which take up so much energy and head space.

A key goal for those of you vulnerable to being groomed and subsequently targeted, is to become better equipped to identify an incident of grooming for what it is – a calculated behaviour or set of behaviours designed to test how effective you are at retaining your power under pressure – so that you can react with a self-protective strategy of your own, one which leaves the would-be bully in no doubt that they would be unwise to select you as a candidate to target.

In Chapter 2 I suggested that the combination of a factor internal to the bully, along with a situational factor in the environment, create the impetus to bully. Let's consider an example of team grooming, and highlight how these two factors play out in the scenario.

- A supervisor of a team in an insurance firm observes one of his peers and workplace friends gaining a bonus for his outstanding performance. The supervisor has worked hard over the previous six months, handling challenging team and client issues with diligence and some degree of skill. While he had been verbally commended by his manager, he had not been offered a bonus. On hearing that his popular and talented peer has received a bonus, initially he feels angry. Over the next few days his anger hardens into resentment towards his employer and then into jealousy towards his peer, and he determines to groom him to see how far he can push him. During a lull in the conversation towards the end of a long meeting involving his peer and three other team colleagues, the jealous supervisor turns towards his peer. Employing a low-key and understated tone, he suggests to him that he would be a more effective team member if in future he is less slow to offer support to people he works with and quicker to appreciate their good work. In the silence which follows, each of the other three team members carefully watches the evolving interaction between the two peers. The peer to whom this remark is addressed takes a deep breath on hearing these unexpected words. While he could not have anticipated that his erstwhile friend would have made these comments, he knows exactly what is happening. Quick as a flash, using an empathic tone, he completely deflates his colleague's attack by saying: 'I guess you must be really disappointed to be overlooked for a bonus.'

In this example, the situational context for the supervisor's decision to groom his peer is the fact that his peer, rather than himself, has gained a degree of kudos and organisational reward which the supervisor believes he also deserves. The internal factor behind his decision to groom his colleague is the fact that, in response to these circumstances, he conceives jealousy towards his colleague and resentment towards his employer, a twin motivator which in his mind justifies his grooming of his peer.

The jealous peer does not confront his own strong disappointment at not being offered a bonus. He does not speak with his manager about what he could do differently and better to secure a bonus in the future. He does not use his energy, determination and talents to build a level of performance which would make it likely – or even inevitable – that he would receive a bonus for outstanding performance in the near future. Instead, he uses his energy to nurture his resentment towards his colleague. Then, in an attempt to destroy some of his peer's current prestige and enjoyment of his bonus, he grooms him in front of three other colleagues. His jealousy crystallises during a meeting between them and three other team members, in an incident of team grooming.

The jealous peer suggests to his colleague in a low-key and apparently neutral tone, that his performance would be enhanced if he was less slow to offer support around the office to his colleagues, and quicker to acknowledge their good work. His tactic in this incident of grooming is an understated barb, one which is calculated to take clear strengths of his colleague – his generous nature and ready ability to coach and collaborate around the office – and characterise them as non-existent. The surprise nature of the grooming by a workplace friend, who up until that moment had been his ally, could have made it difficult for the generous peer to react effectively in the moment. In addition, the encounter is being observed by three other team members, none of whom outwardly reacts to the barbed comment or appears to support him as he responds to it. Nonetheless, the generous peer is wise and he sees the tactic for what it is: an attempt to groom him in a team meeting. He deflects the subliminal aggression with his well-chosen and pithy reply: 'I guess you must be really disappointed to be looked over for a bonus.'

This comment is effective because it cuts right to the heart of the matter. It puts the issues back to the would-be bully, placing on the table the true motives behind the jealous peer's attack. His exact wording is important. He does not say: 'You must be disappointed that I got a bonus and you didn't.' Nor does he say: 'You sound jealous' or 'You are jealous!' Instead, he unmasks the jealous peer while simultaneously putting and keeping the spotlight on him. The jealous peer can no longer hide from his own internal landscape. His true feelings consist of a powerful sense of disappointment at being overlooked for a financial reward, which he has allowed to crystallise into jealousy. This fact is now on the table, having been placed there by the colleague he just tried to groom. Everyone else in the room can see the truth too, and each of them will be wary of this side of the jealous peer's character in the future. The jealous peer had hoped to incite all or some of these three people to support him, whether tacitly or openly. His generous peer's clever response to being groomed precluded either of these responses, as all three by-standers now also know that he is too self-protecting to be groomed that easily. They also have just witnessed an effective role-model for how to neutralise an incident of grooming.

The jealous peer now has a choice. Does he decide to face his own disappointment and re-commit to do his best for his employer? Or does he continue to snipe at a generous peer who has already proven himself more than a match for his jealous nature?

Putting the Issues Back to the Bully

As we have just seen, finding something influential to say involves *putting the issues back to the bully at the time of an incident of grooming.* Finding something influential to say is a self-protective thing to do in the moment of being groomed because it changes the dynamic evolving between you, switching the focus away from you and putting it back to the would-be bully. Part of the power of the generous peer's words in the above example lies in *what he says*. Part of it lies in *how he says them*. Using a clear and relaxed tone with a hint of empathy he shows the would-be bully that he knows how to retain his composure under pressure, and is choosing to be kind to him even under attack. While it is not always appropriate to respond to grooming with empathy, in this scenario it added to the influence of the generous peer's rejoinder because it demonstrated to the bully that the generous peer *retains absolute control over his behaviour and choices at the time of the grooming, even to the point of being kind*. For the generous peer, in that incident with that bully, it was an assertive thing to do.

Some incidents of grooming involve subtle, covert forms of bullying aggression. Others involve more obvious, outright and open aggression. Should you be subject to any of these forms of grooming, it is important that you respond in the moment because this is the optimal time to alter in your favour the bullying dynamic the would-be bully is trying to create. Take a deep breath. Compose yourself. Then reply to the grooming behaviour using a factual, unemotional tone which tells the would-be bully that you know how to handle yourself.

Consider the following examples:

- During a relaxed team lunch, a would-be bully turns to his target and says to her: 'You don't really fit in round here, do you?' Although she wants one of her colleagues to leap to her defence, the target quickly realises that none of them is going to. She takes a deep breath and in a composed tone says: 'What do you mean?'

- During a lull in a weekly team briefing meeting, the would-be bully turns to her target and says: 'I'm surprised at how quiet you are being. I had the impression that you were quite confident in meetings.' The target is initially stung and confused. She regains her composure and says: 'That *is* how I am in meetings. I speak when I have something worthwhile to say. How about you?'

- During a tense team meeting called by the team leader to discuss recent client criticism of an important report, a would-be bully turns to her target and says: 'Well, you dropped us right in it!' The target is initially thrown at being scapegoated as he knows he had only a marginal role in the creation of the report. He is embarrassed and hurt at being singled out in this unfair way in the middle of an awkward meeting. He regains his poise and, in a lull in the conversation, turns towards the would-be bully and puts her into a neat double-bind. He says: 'As we both know, I had an insignificant role in writing that report. I heard what you said just then to mean that you were trying to shift blame onto me, which can't be right. So, run it past me again. What did you just say?' This double bind places the bully in a position where she can't easily repeat what she has just said when invited to re-phrase. If she does, she'll look a fool in front of the team. The truth is on the table (the target said he had minimal input to the report), everyone in the team heard him say it, and he has given the bully a chance to redeem herself by re-phrasing. His invitation to re-phrase is so skilful that the bully can avoid embarrassment this time round. But, the bully has also been given a warning: that this target knows their own mind, can stand their ground with considerable skill, and is able to draw the line when they want to.

In each of the above examples, the would-be bully grooms their team colleague to see how they handle the attack. Each of these incidents occurs in front of other team members, allowing the would-be bully to assess how robust their target is when everyone else in the team is present and they are put under the spotlight. None of the targets likes being attacked in front of their team, but none of them is silenced by the attack. In each case, the response of the target to the grooming is effective because it simultaneously:

- Puts the issues back to the bully.

- Clarifies the boundary between the facts and the misinformation which the would-be bully is promoting.

- Lays down the clear marker that the target has not been thrown by the grooming, and is not rendered vulnerable by it.

Should you be groomed, it is important that you find something to say at the time which alters the dynamic the would-be bully is trying to create between you. Tactics you could employ include:

- *Asking the bully what they mean if their grooming tactic consists of being indirect or evasive.* This tactic requires the bully to cease using innuendo or insinuation and be clear about what they are saying. Examples of effective questions include: 'What are you talking about?' or 'What does that mean?' or 'What do you mean by that comment?'

- *Directly disagreeing with the bully if what they are saying is dishonest or untrue.* This tells them that you know your own mind and are unafraid to say so. It demonstrates that you will not sit silent while they misrepresent you or your behaviour. An example would be the situation in which a bully wants to highlight a strength of yours and reduce it to a weakness or liability. In this case, you could say: 'I don't see myself like that.'

- *Challenging the bully's perception of you if they are trying to characterise you unkindly or unfairly.* This tells them that you know the difference between truth and falsehood, and can quite easily clarify the distinction between the two. It also tells them that your self-image is your business, and they cannot negatively affect the way you see yourself. An example would be the situation in which a bully wants to characterise you as lacking in relationship-building skills. In this case, you could say: 'One of my strengths is that I am quick to build rapport.'

A persistent would-be bully won't necessary be put off by rejoinders like these. They may well try to groom you again, either straightaway or on another occasion, to test your resolve. But some would-be bullies will desist immediately they recognise that they are dealing with someone who is resolute and skilled enough to hold their own.

Should you be subject to persistent grooming, simply maintain your composure and continue to put the issues back to the would-be bully until they desist. By doing this, in the same unruffled and calm manner, you will send back the clear message that you are not going to be an easy target for them, that they can keep trying to groom you if they want to, but you are more than a match for them.

Mishandling an Incident of Team Grooming

Potential targets often mishandle grooming incidents and become vulnerable to subsequent bullying because, understandably, they feel confused about what happened during the grooming incident. It is vital that you recognise the moment for what it is should you be subject to grooming behaviour, and avoid remaining silent and submissive. The fact that you feel confused and vulnerable *is* the signal that what occurred was problematic. Let's explore some of the factors which might result in you remaining silent instead of responding influentially to an incident of grooming. You may:

- *Mentally make an excuse for the would-be bully:* you may put their grooming behaviour down to them having a bad day or, worse still from a self-protective point of view, you may think you have done something wrong which warrants the aggression you were subject to. In either of these cases, you may let the moment pass, fail to confront the grooming either at the time or immediately afterwards and, crucially, not adjust your demeanour around the would-be bully the next time you have an encounter with them making it easier for them to attack you a second time.

- *Allow your confusion to render you silent:* you may feel confused about what just happened. Not understanding how a team colleague could attack you is completely understandable. But allowing your confusion to dominate your behaviour and render you silent is unwise. It means that you fail to protect yourself, making it much easier for that colleague to groom you again.

- *Fail to ask the obvious question:* you may be unable to ask the obvious question, such as 'what does that mean?' or 'what did you just say?' and miss the opportunity to confront. Questions like these require the would-be bully to give account and makes it clear that while you might have been initially thrown by what they said, you are not floored by it and can confront.

- *Choose to avoid confronting the grooming out of a fear that if you do respond the incident will escalate:* this is an understandable fear to have, and is prevalent among those of you who struggle to use assertive behaviour. It is true that a poorly constructed, emotional response will not work well for you. A skilled would-be bully would likely turn your self-doubt and uncertainty against you. But it is not actually true that confrontation always leads to escalation. A carefully crafted, self-protective response *will* give the would-be bully pause for thought, and will completely stop many bullies. Acknowledge that you feel uncertain and on the back foot. Take a breath. And then engage with the grooming behaviour.

Trusting Your Inner Wisdom

I take the view that you have answers to your dilemmas inside you, even if you might be unable to access your inner wisdom for a time due to your confusion or distress. Should you be subject to an incident of grooming, what you need is a safe place to unpack your confusion so that you can come to your own conclusions about what happened, and what you need to do going forward.

If you have been groomed and left disoriented by the interaction with a would-be bully, whether or not you managed to put the issues back to the bully at the time of the incident, one of your concerns is likely to be what might happen the next time you meet that colleague. Those of you very concerned about your next encounter with a skilful workplace groomer may generate so much anxiety that you start to avoid your adversary and don't go to meetings which you might otherwise go to. In this case, your anxiety could set you up for a situation in which you might not perform to standard because you are missing vital meetings, and in which you become afraid of the groomer's 'power' over you. To detoxify from the grooming encounter you need to step back from it, look at it objectively and rationally, and ask yourself questions to enable you to come to your own conclusions about how to handle that colleague differently and better. The questions at the end of this chapter will help you do just that.

Let's now see how the themes of this chapter play out in a longer example.

Case Study 4: First Impressions

A small design company moves offices into a renovated mill, as a result of which the eight young, amiable and enthusiastic members of the workforce start to share one open-plan office. This represents a significant change for them, as in their old premises, each of the team members had their own office albeit some of them were inter-connected. The entire team is excited about the move. They enjoy working in the small, involving and tight-knit team, and expect to like working in their new premises. Under the new desk arrangements, the four designers will share the same space as the saleswoman, the two team PAs and the owner of the business. In preparation for an expanded portfolio which they hope to create, the business owner hires an experienced marketing specialist who is to start work at the end of the first week in the new premises.

Two weeks into their occupancy of their new location the sales-woman and business owner leave mid-morning to meet a potential client. The remaining seven people meet to have their lunch together, albeit a couple of them bring their work diaries and paperwork with them. They sit around the conference room table at one end of the large open-plan space. Nothing untoward occurs during the opening minutes of the conversation, with different people remarking on the ease or otherwise of their journey, their liking for the light and airy space, and their pleasure at the informal and friendly atmosphere they have created already. Then, in an act of apparent clumsiness, the marketing specialist knocks over a cup of coffee which flows across the table, over the paperwork and then onto the skirt of one of the PAs. In the flurry of activity which greets this incident different members of the team grab handfuls of paper towels, offer sympathy and help her mop up the mess. Throughout this process, the market-ing specialist continues to eat his lunch but doesn't make any remark about what happened. Indeed, he barely looks up from his food. So intent is everyone else in the team at remedying the situation, that they appear not to notice that the marketing specialist has not referred to or apologised for his clumsiness. As the lunch hour con-cludes, the team members get up from the table and head towards their desks. As he steps past her, the marketing manager bumps into the other PA, treading on her toes and causing her to stumble in full view of everyone else. Once more, he does not acknowledge the fact and proceeds on his way as if the incident had not occurred.

Over the next week, the marketing specialist arranges a series of one-to-one meetings with each PA, and with each of the four designers. At the conclusion of each meeting, these team members seem downcast, carry a strained expression and find it hard to concentrate on their work for the next hour or so. Although none of them wants to say anything to any of their colleagues for fear of being regarded as an office gossip, it is clear that the atmosphere in the team has altered. The light-hearted banter and enjoyment of working together has gone. Instead, team members come to work with a heavy heart, work more slowly and spend more time alone, going out to lunch separately rather than eating together. The two most senior members of the business, the saleswoman and the owner, feel under significant pressure to bring in additional business to pay for the new employee and are out of the office with clients most of the time. On the odd occasion when they come into the office, they are too preoccupied to notice that something is wrong.

First Impressions: Analysing the Team Dynamics

Let's analyse the dynamics which play out between the marketing specialist and the members of the team he has joined to clarify the dynamics in these two incidents of team grooming, and what their adversary learns from the way the team members handle the incidents.

From his earliest dealings with his new team members at lunch one week into his new job, the marketing specialist is on the look-out for opportunities to treat his colleagues with discourtesy, disdain and a degree of rudeness that is quite out of character in a team where people get along well and enjoy working together. His initial grooming takes the form of knocking a cup of coffee over one of the PAs, something he does without even glancing in her direction let alone acknowledging what he has done or apologising to her. He remains aloof from the rushed attempts made by her colleagues to assist her, and doesn't involve himself in those activities at all. As the lunch concludes, he grooms again. He deliberately jostles the second PA, treading on her foot as he walks away from the lunch table, again failing to acknowledge or apologise for his actions. Had he done so on both occasions, he could have passed the incidents off as accidental. But the fact that he doesn't say anything about them is what is so troubling. Both incidents were personal to the PAs in that they involved actions which impacted them physically. Both incidents also provide clear evidence of a level of derision on the part of the marketing specialist and, crucially, both enable him to carefully observe how everyone else present at the time responds to his grooming behaviour. He learns that the targets and their team colleagues are not willing to hold him accountable or to confront him. *They effectively let him get away with it.*

In the first grooming incident, he learns that everyone hurries to help the PA with her soaked paperwork and skirt. But he also learns that all the team members overlook his deliberate actions, assuming them to be unintentional or accidental. No one reprimands him, directs a pointed comment at him or even questions him about what has happened. The absence of any of these behaviours encourages him to proceed with his second grooming, something which he does straight after the meal. This time he grooms the second PA, targeting her as she walks away from the table. Although everyone leaves at the same time, she is walking alone. Again, there is no come-back as neither she nor anyone nearby says anything directly to him, again choosing to pass off what he did as clumsiness and not deliberate. The degree of reluctance to confront displayed by the team does not do them any favours at all. That in no way removes responsibility from the marketing specialist for two clear instances of grooming designed to see how far he can push members of the team. Having ascertained that he can push them a long way, he then commences his campaigns of team bullying against all of them during a series of one-to-one meetings. He attacks every team member personally and professionally, leaving them crumpled and deflated.

The marketing specialist grooms the two PAs in full view of the entire team in two carefully chosen and well-executed instances. His observation of both instances encourages him that neither of his two targets, nor the other team members, is likely to resist him if he commences a campaign against the entire team. Although we do not know what he subsequently says to each person in their one-to-one meetings, we can surmise by their changed demeanour after meeting with him, that he successfully targets them, injuring them both personally and professionally. On leaving their encounter with him, each person is obviously flattened which strongly suggests that he undermines their ability to carry out their work and undermines their self-esteem and self-confidence. The character of the previously happy, friendly and productive team is changed dramatically as team colleagues keep themselves to themselves, don't eat lunch together, and work less well together.

First Impressions: Conclusions

What conclusions can we draw from this case study? Firstly, we can say that the two targets and the other team members who witnessed the incidents of grooming, mishandled both moments *due to their inability to see what was really happening.* Their good-natured amiability results in each person who observed the two incidents of grooming mishandling the moments, ascribing benign clumsiness to their new colleague on both occasions. On neither occasion were the marketing specialist's intentions benign. Both incidents of grooming were conducted by him on the first day that his employer and the other senior member of the workforce were out of the office, in deliberate calculated manoeuvres. His intention was to groom the two most junior members of the workforce in hierarchical terms, the two PAs, in full view of everyone else in the team, in a social situation over lunch when everyone was off-guard and relaxed. His strategy was to use physical aggression in the form of apparent clumsiness to see how his new colleagues responded to the behaviour. Given that they couldn't see into the mind of the marketing specialist, what clues were available to the team in order that they might interpret his behaviour more astutely? Whilst it was reasonable for them initially to put the drink spillage down to an accident, concerns should have arisen in their minds when the marketing specialist failed to show any care for the colleague he had just soaked. Instead they made the mistake of *ignoring something that was in plain sight and failing to ask the obvious question about it.* Again, it is understandable that these good-natured team members initially chose to view the injury to the PA's toe as a second unfortunate accident, but they did not pick up on the fact that the marketing specialist failed to show any concern for the person he had injured. Once again, the team members chose to ignore the marketing specialist's disregard for his colleague's welfare and failed to challenge him. And that is exactly what the would-be bully wanted: evidence that his team colleagues were prepared to ignore obvious red flags and thereby present themselves as straightforward targets for a subsequent campaign.

Secondly, we can say that over lunch the existing members of the team were presented with two clear opportunities to draw sound conclusions about the true character of their new colleague, *but they ignored the obvious warning signs.* The marketing specialist's behaviour had an adverse physical impact on two of his colleagues: his cold-hearted disregard for each of them had been plain for all to see, and in those moments, he revealed his true nature. Had he apologised, seemed flustered or offered some act of contrition, then his team colleagues would have known he had not intended anything untoward by his actions. But the *absence of an apology or any attempt to make recompense for either of his acts of grooming is a clear signal that something is wrong.* It is a clear signal that the existing team members need to heed. Had they given proper weight to the fact that their new colleague had twice failed to take responsibility for his apparent clumsiness, then they could have drawn the specific, firm conclusion that, however hard it will be for them to accept, their new colleague did these things deliberately. Sadly for them, they ignored the clear warning signs and ascribed more benign but untrue motives to their new colleague.

Thirdly, we can say that by letting the two grooming incidents pass without comment, the team members left themselves vulnerable to further attacks from a callous and skilled assailant. The would-be bully's grooming is evidence of a degree of ruthlessness which is surprising for a new employee, and partly accounts for why the existing team members are taken so much by surprise. They make the mistake of assuming that he, like they, would want to fit in. Consequently, they don't draw attention to his, as they see it, unfortunate and potentially embarrassing faux-pas over lunch. They completely fail to see that he is not at all embarrassed. In fact, he is quite calm and unconcerned that he has knocked coffee all over one of his new colleague's paperwork and clothing. Subsequently, he is not at all bothered that he steps on the foot of another new colleague. In both cases, the team members witnessing these acts of grooming misunderstand the motive behind them. They make a serious error of judgement by not ascribing a more malign motive to the marketing specialist.

Lastly, we can say that in order to avoid being targeted in the subsequent campaign, the team members present at lunch need to confront the would-be bully clearly and firmly. Given their desire for harmony and their conflict-averse natures, they need to do this in a way which is congruent with these values. On noticing that their new colleague doesn't offer to help the PA clear up the spilled coffee, one of them could ask: 'Didn't you see what you just did?' The form of this question is important. It makes a direct link between the *actions of the new employee and the outcome of those actions,* effectively holding him accountable for them. This is quite different from either: 'Didn't you see what just happened?' or 'Aren't you going to help?' Neither of these two questions *holds the culprit responsible.* They both draw attention to what just happened and to the consequences for the PA struggling with spilled coffee. But neither of these two questions puts the issues back to the would-be bully, or requires him to answer for his actions. The question 'Didn't you see what you just did?' does both these things. It simultaneously tells the would-be bully that his behaviour has been noted, that it is not acceptable for him to fail to address what he just did, and that he now has to account for that behaviour. Should the would-be bully fail to answer the question and simply keep on eating his lunch without concern for the PA, then the team has a decision to make. Do they continue to eat lunch with a new member of the workforce who has just demonstrated an unusual degree of disdain for them? Or do they quietly but decidedly leave the room, removing themselves from an invidious situation, and return to their work? The latter course of action would have prevented the second incident of grooming and would have made it clear to the would-be bully that they may be kind-hearted but they also know where the line is. As it is they chose the first option, setting the second PA up for a subsequent incident of grooming, and setting themselves up for a campaign of team bullying in which all of them are targeted.

Summary of Key Points from the Chapter

Team grooming is the behaviour which occurs before a campaign of team bullying occurs. It is the would-be bully's way of assessing the degree to which you are vulnerable to being successfully targeted. Some incidents of team grooming occur during one-to-one encounters with the would-be bully. In these cases, the bully is on the look-out for evidence of vulnerability, confusion or self-doubt on your part. Some incidents of team grooming occur in front of some or all of your team colleagues. In this case, the bully is also observing how these people respond to the grooming:

with a verbal retort, with support for you or with passivity and submission.

Responding effectively to grooming involves finding something to say which simultaneously puts the issues back to the bully while also holding them to account. You could ask a question, make a statement or directly disagree with them, but your aim is to use a clear and relaxed tone to convey that you have not been flustered by the grooming incident and know how to protect yourself.

Many would-be bullies will desist immediately when they realise that you know how to handle yourself. They desist because these bullies only use the room for manoeuvre that you inadvertently give them. Other bullies will respond to an assertive rejoinder by trying to groom you a second or third time. In these cases, they are testing your resolve. It is important that, once groomed by a team colleague, you maintain your clear and resolute approach in every encounter you have with them thereafter until they get the message and stop grooming you.

Your inner wisdom is your ally should you be subject to team grooming. The very fact that you feel confused and thrown by the behaviour *is* the warning you need to heed. Incidents of grooming are never an accident. Nor are they justifiable. Don't fall into the trap of making an excuse for the would-be bully, or downplaying their behaviour because you think it would be easier to overlook it than to deal with it. Taking this line will leave you vulnerable to repeated incidents of grooming and expose you to the probability of being subject to a campaign.

If you are groomed in front of your team, the whole team bears a responsibility for confronting the would-be bully. Team members who avoid this responsibility, or who do not recognise the need to confront in the first place, make it much easier for bullies to commence their campaign against you, while also giving their own power away to the bully.

Questions for You to Consider

In this chapter, we have been examining grooming in your team. You may now want to apply this material to your own experience by responding to the following questions. You can jot down your answer to each in the space below it.

Call to mind an incident in which you were subject to grooming in your team.

1. What happened during this grooming incident?

2. What did the would-be bully do and say that you found confusing or which rendered you vulnerable?

3. What was the most confusing thing about the interaction at the time?

4. What troubled you most about it?

5. Looking back on it now, what could you have said or done at the time which would have put the issues back to the would-be bully?

6. Which, if any, of your team colleagues was present at the time of the grooming? How did they react?

7. What impact did their reaction have on the would-be bully at the time of the grooming and subsequently?

Next Chapter

Chapter 5 expands on the themes introduced in this chapter on grooming by discussing how to respond effectively to bullying behaviour during a campaign against you. The chapter focuses on the team bullying dynamic that the bully wants to create in the team, exploring what it is and how it operates, and highlights the key skills and principles involved in handling an incident of team bullying effectively at the moment of attack. This chapter illustrates how your response (as the target), and your team colleagues' response (as witnesses to the bullying), influence the way in which the bullying dynamic evolves from that moment onwards. The chapter also highlights the subtle but powerful alterations the bully wants to encourage in existing team relationships, and how the actions of the non-targeted team members can thwart their plans just as much as judicious responses from you, the target.

Chapter 5
Responding Effectively to
Team Bullying

The Team Bullying Dynamic

At the heart of any team bullying campaign is the bully's desire to create a team bullying dynamic. The team bullying dynamic operates both in the bully's relationship with you, their target, and in their relationship with the wider team. The team bullying dynamic is about the bully's desire to alter the balance of power between you and the bully, and between the bully and other members of the team. Consequently, there are two different but interconnected strands to the team bullying dynamic:

- The patterns of behaviour which are set up between you, the target, and the bully which keep you on the back foot and to some extent keep the bully in charge of the interactions between you.

- The altered power dynamics in the wider team in which allegiances shift, as team members who are not direct targets of the campaign decide whom to ally with: the bully, you or, in their minds, neutrality.

The bully wants to create a team dynamic whereby, for the length of the campaign against you, they can retain as much control as possible over you and other members of the team, effectively swaying the balance of power in their direction. A team bully will attempt to set up a team bullying dynamic which comprises:

- Your passive or submissive outward reaction to their hostility at the time of an attack – a pattern of behaviour that the bully wants to become the norm between the two of you during the campaign against you.

- Your team colleagues becoming disconcerted, anxious or afraid such that they defer to, collude with or ignore the bullying behaviour, thereby giving further power to the bully.

A skilled bully whose behaviour has put you, the target, onto the back foot can leave you feeling that:

- You have few or no behavioural choices at the time of an attack.

- The bully has all the power in the interaction between you.

- You have to comply with their will.

Equally, a skilled bully who has successfully created a team bullying dynamic, can leave some or all of your team colleagues feeling:

- *Uncertain around the bully.* Their uncertainty may result in them being cautious or treading on egg shells when they interact with the bully, for fear of provoking an attack against themselves.

- *Uncomfortable around you.* Their discomfort may be connected to their knowledge that you are being targeted and their inability to do anything decisive about it.

- *Self-doubting and conflicted.* Colleagues who do not take an obvious stand against the bullying may either actively comply with the bully or fail to offer you support at the time of an attack, or afterwards. Any of these reactions could result in them feeling that they have made an unhealthy choice, even though they remain committed to that course of action.

- *Anxious and afraid.* Their anxiety and fear may be a result of their concern that they might also be attacked.

- *Shame-faced and angry.* Their shame may be directed towards themselves because they know that they are enabling bullying by their passivity and submission. But even though they feel ashamed of their own behaviour, they may direct their consequent anger towards you. Why might they do this? Because it is easier and safer for them to be angry with you, the target of the bully's attacks, than it is for them to be angry with the bully themselves.

These dynamics are especially pernicious if the bully has greater organisational authority than you and your colleagues, perhaps because they are the team's immediate manager or their boss. In this case, a combination of factors can leave you, the target, and to some extent your team colleagues, feeling beleaguered, with no way out. These include the bully's:

- Organisational status

- Skill at using coercive behaviour

- Ability to alter the balance of power in the team in their favour

To a compliant target who lacks the know-how or the energy to find effective ways of handling the bullying at the time of an attack, these dynamics can feel as if they are set in stone. But these dynamics are *not* set in stone. You have much more influence than you realise. *What you say and do at the time of an attack influences the way the team bullying dynamic evolves between you and the bully. What your team colleagues say and do at the time of attacks they witness influences the way the team bullying dynamic evolves around them.* While most team bullies will not outwardly display discomfort or run away, they do wobble internally when confronted effectively in the moment of an attack and, in those moments, the balance of power shifts away from them. Why? Because they no longer have the degree of control they feel they need.

When the team bully is a senior manager, an important fee earner or when they carry out any other influential role in the organisation, the pressures are compounded for you and your team. But the truth is that, even though the bully has more *organisational power* than you, you have access to the same degree of *personal power* that they do. However limited, you, the target, and your team colleagues, *always have the choice about how you behave, what you believe, what you say and what you do at the time of an attack.* The wise exercising of these choices at the time of an attack *is* the personal power available to you, and exercising these choices *does* alter the bullying dynamic in your favour. Sometimes this alteration may be a decisive shift in your favour, and at other times it may only be sufficient to enable you to manage that encounter. Exercising your right to make a choice in the moment of an attack *does* alter the bullying dynamic, and puts the team bully onto the back foot. Why? Because the team bully is no longer in control of your actions or your team colleagues' actions. You are. And your colleagues are.

Let's explore how the themes of this chapter play out in a longer example.

Case Study 5: Singled Out

The sales team from an engineering firm attend a networking event organised by one of their largest customers. The sales team consists of three men and one woman. None of them likes networking, each of them experiencing it as both draining and outside their comfort zone. Nevertheless, they are determined to make the most of the opportunity to meet potential new customers and cement relationships with existing customers.

During the first half-hour of the meeting, the members of the sales team stick together. They each purchase a drink from the bar, and join a circle of four people they don't know standing nearby. The female member of the team finds herself talking to a tall man who introduces himself as the buyer from a large car manufacturer. The female team member is immediately on the alert to the possibility of a fruitful conversation with a potential new customer. She speaks with him knowledgeably about the engineering firm's range of products, service specifications and quality assurance criteria. Encouraged by the buyer's steady eye contact and occasional nods of the head, she thinks about introducing him to the other members of the team. She signals to the nearest of her team colleagues, motioning him to join her, and as he does so she makes the introductions. She then motions to her two other colleagues to join her, and soon the four of them are talking with the potential buyer.

Aware that the female team member is standing on his right, the buyer starts to speak animatedly with the salesman on his left. He talks loudly and at pace, without making obvious eye contact with any of the other members of the sales team, who begin to talk amongst themselves. Shortly afterwards, he puts his drink down to enable him to move his hands more expansively. In the course of a particularly vigorous hand gesture, he jostles the female team member in the mid-riff. She bridles and takes half-a-step backwards, but doesn't otherwise comment on the incident.

A few minutes later, after concluding his conversation with the salesmen standing next to him, the potential buyer turns back to the female team member on his other side. Leaving the three male team members to talk among themselves, he leans in towards her, loosens his tie and says: 'I ought to arrange for you to be attacked on your way to your car.' The female team member is shocked and goes cold. She feels totally thrown. Her initial thought is that she must have misheard the buyer as he couldn't possible have said that he ought to arrange for her to be attacked on the way to her car. Astonished that he could have apparently threatened her in the middle of a networking meeting in front of her entire team, she stares at him, her mind blank and her expression frozen. In the silence which follows, she realises that his cold expression and chilling eyes are entirely congruent with a threat to her physical safety.

Aware of his cold penetrating gaze, and deeply discomforted by it, the female saleswoman half-turns away from him towards her colleagues. Instantly aware that something is wrong, they stop talking and look in her direction. Having secured their attention, she turns back to the buyer and says in a firm and factual tone: 'You just said you ought to arrange for me to be attacked on the way to my car.'

The buyer throws his head back, scoffs, and says: 'Come, come. I was joking. Can't you take a joke?' The female team member responds with another firm and clear reply. Still looking at him, and aware that her colleagues are following every word, using a factual tone she says: 'It didn't sound like a joke.' The female team member then breaks eye contact with the buyer, turns to face her colleagues, and remains outwardly composed with her shoulders back. She waits for someone to speak. One of her male colleagues takes up the challenge and directs a comment at her. He says that he had an interesting discussion with a new contact a few minutes ago, and would like to introduce the two of them. A second colleague chips in with a comment about how the female saleswoman's knowledge of the market would be useful for the upcoming introduction. The four colleagues move away together, leaving the buyer by himself. The female saleswoman is shaken and disturbed, but is bolstered by the active support of her colleagues. The buyer remains standing where he is for a few minutes, aloof and alone. Then he jolts himself out of his reverie and walks stiffly out of the meeting.

Singled Out: Analysing the Team Dynamics

Let's analyse the dynamics which play out between the buyer, the female saleswoman and the three male team members during the networking meeting. We will pay particular attention to the team bullying dynamic which the buyer tries to inculcate, and the way in which the effective responses of the target and her wider team nullify his attack.

In this example, a sales team of one woman and three men attends a networking meeting. Soon after arriving, the female team member falls into conversation with a buyer from a car manufacturing firm and, after speaking knowledgeably with him for a few minutes, invites her team colleagues to join her. The buyer is an arrogant man. He is also a misogynist. He assumes that the female team member must be the weakest member of the team, and persists in this view even though she speaks to him with authority and experience about the engineering products and services her company offers. He also assumes that her male colleagues must disrespect her too, a set of conclusions which encourages him to groom her straightaway and see how all of them handle the incident. He fully expects the male members of the team to either defer to his status as a potential customer, collude with him against her, or turn a blind eye. The way will then be open for him to create a team bullying dynamic among members of a sales team looking to work with him.

His act of grooming involves him jostling the saleswoman in the midriff while apparently enjoying an animated conversation with one of her colleagues. The female team member takes half-a-step backwards but doesn't verbally confront him, and none of the other team members reacts to the grooming either. The buyer concludes that the way is open for him to move swiftly to an attack against the female team member, and he commences his campaign straightaway. He completely misjudges both her and her team colleagues.

The buyer turns towards the female team member, signalling that he wants to talk to her alone. Her colleagues take the hint and speak among themselves. The buyer's attack is astonishing, a threat against her physical safety uttered straightaway without pre-amble. True, the saleswoman and the entire team have just been groomed and she could reasonably expect some degree of untoward behaviour from the buyer along with the continuation of their previous sales discussion. But she does not expect the shocking turn which the conversation takes. As she hears this threat to her physical safety, the saleswoman goes into shock and immediately doubts herself. She thinks that the buyer could not possibly have said: 'I ought to arrange for you to be attacked on your way to your car.' She looks into his eyes and sees his chilling cold gaze. She realises that he did say those words and that she needs to act quickly and decisively. What does she say and do that is so effective at protecting herself, and gives her colleagues the opportunity to work with her to prevent a team bullying dynamic being created between them and the buyer?

- *She makes sure she has witnesses to her confrontation.* In the split second she has to make up her mind, the saleswoman decides she cannot confront the buyer in private, even though his attack was verbalised as a quiet aside to her alone. Instead, she makes what he said public, completely altering the bullying dynamic he was trying to create. The buyer had hoped that by attacking her in a conversation between the two of them, he could intimidate her to such an extent that she would be unable to defend herself effectively. But by making his words public, she takes back her power in an instant and leaves him with the job of having to defend himself.

- *She plays his words straight back to him in exactly the form he said them.* The female team member adopts a serious expression and says in a clear factual tone: 'You just said you ought to arrange for me to be attacked on the way to my car.' This is a clever thing to do because *it places the buyer and his conduct under the spotlight in front of her three team colleagues* and cuts down the room he has for manoeuvre. Had she simply said 'You just threatened me' or 'What did you say that for?' the buyer would not have been unmasked for the duplicitous and callous character he is, because none of her colleagues would have known what he had said. Either of these rejoinders, or any variation of them, would also have played right into the buyer's hands, enabling him *to make the saleswoman's reaction the problem rather than what he just said.* As soon as the female team member repeats exactly what he said in full hearing of her team colleagues, the buyer is the one on the back foot.

- *She speaks with conviction, in a firm and factual tone that leaves no room for doubt.* The female team member uses a factual and firm tone throughout her confrontation, without a hint of a smile to soften her challenge. She does not sound emotional or upset, although she is quite understandably both. She realises that if she sounds wobbly, her assailant will turn her emotion back on her in a renewed attack. Instead, she puts her shoulders back, holds her head high and tells it like it is in clear, factual and unassailable tones.

- *She refuses to be characterised as a woman who cannot take a joke.* The buyer's initial reaction to having his words made public is to try and characterise them as a joke, an attempt to malign the female team member for lacking a sense of humour. But she will not be wrong-footed that easily. Using the same calm and clear factual tone, she tells him that what he said did not sound like a joke. She puts the fact of the matter on the table: she heard his words as a direct threat to her physical safety and she is calling him on it.

- *Having confronted him, she breaks eye contact, allowing other members of her team to have the opportunity to speak.* She stands with her shoulders back and a composed expression on her face, waiting for someone to speak. She cannot know who will speak next, or what they will say, but she hopes that someone from her team will say something.

At this point in the incident, the female team member has defended herself admirably against the misogynistic buyer. But the team is still not out of the woods. From this point onwards, what the other team members say and do is important in finally thwarting the team bullying dynamic that the buyer is trying to create. He has been unable to intimidate the female team member during or after his attack on her physical safety. What actions do the male members of the team take that ultimately prove decisive in preventing a team bullying dynamic being created?

- *Her first colleague communicates to the female team member that he would like to remove her from the situation.* Her colleague does this by saying that he had earlier been speaking to someone who he would like to introduce her to. This statement makes it clear to the buyer that the female team member's *personal safety* is important to him, and that this particular sales discussion is now closed.

- *Her second colleague tells her that her experience of the market would be useful in that discussion.* This statement tells the buyer that a second member of her team is also actively supporting the female team member, and makes it clear to the buyer that the sales woman is regarded as *a valued member of the team.*

- *None of the male team members pays any attention to the buyer.* They withdraw from his company with their female colleague, leaving the buyer standing alone and defeated. This tells the buyer that they are not at all impressed by his status as a possible major customer or the possibility of doing business with him, that they are willing to forego the income they could have earned for their employer by working with him, and that they are making the clear choice to stand against his bullying behaviour. They close ranks around their bullied colleague in a professional and low-key way, and walk away.

The female team member is badly shaken by these events, but she is not injured by them. Her own skill at the moment of attack, and her colleagues' unequivocal support straight after the threat to her physical safety, mitigates the trauma she might otherwise have felt at being threatened with assault at a networking meeting.

Singled Out: Conclusions

What conclusions can we draw from this scenario? Firstly, we can say that the female team member handles her confrontation with the buyer in a way which is highly effective. *She achieves her success as much by what she does not do, as by what she does do.* What she does do is hold her head up high, put her shoulders back and speak in a firm factual tone, a combination which contributes to a powerful confrontation. She appears confident and assertive, even though she might not *feel* it. But, her confrontation works so well because she doesn't undermine her own message with signals that she is on the back foot, vulnerable or scared, or seeking to please or appease. What are the verbal and non-verbal signals which the buyer would interpret as clues indicating that she might be someone he could easily exploit?

These signals include a nervous laugh as she finishes speaking, a small smile part-way through speaking, an inappropriately warm manner, a submissive dip of the head, an apologetic or uncertain tone, wringing her hands, hunching her shoulders or any other sign that she is not fully invested in her personal power. Had she included any of these signals, the female team member would have weakened her confrontation, perhaps ruining it altogether. Happily, she avoids all of these pitfalls and handles the confrontation with authority and skill.

Secondly, we can say that all the team members make the clear choice not to be bullied by a potential major customer even at the expense of losing business they might otherwise have gained. Their decision to walk away from a potential new customer not only protects the target at the networking meeting, it also protects the entire team from future attack. The buyer has already shown himself to be completely unscrupulous, someone willing to try to manipulate established team dynamics for his purpose of gaining a spurious sense of his own supremacy. The team would have placed themselves in an invidious position had they gone ahead and, despite the evidence before them, attempted to secure business from such an unprincipled character.

Thirdly, we can say that their choice to take a firm stand against the bullying was *a self-protective thing for the entire team.* Even with sales bonuses on the line, choosing to sell to someone who has demonstrated himself to be untrustworthy, callous and capable of unusually abhorrent behaviour would inevitably involve setting themselves up for future trouble. Once he had struck a deal with them, and had them in his 'power', the buyer would have plenty of opportunities to dominate, manipulate or otherwise control them, and could easily extend his unscrupulous ways to reneging on the deal at the last minute or bad-mouthing them to other potential customers or any of a number of other scurrilous acts. This customer is not a customer worth dealing with.

Fourthly, we can surmise that the buyer badly miscalculates the characters of the people he is dealing with. His assumption that women are weak, that a woman is out of place in the engineering world, and that her male colleagues would inevitably share his view, were all shown up as the conceits they are. His beliefs that he could control the actions of a team of four people, create enmity between them, remove power from them and place it with himself, were also shown to be unwise precepts to act on. Instead of driving a wedge between the colleagues and exploiting the ensuing rifts, he watches them walk away from him united in their disdain for his behaviour. He is left defeated and alone, his moment of triumph turned against him. After standing by himself for a few minutes, the buyer feels so uncomfortable that he stiffly leaves the meeting.

Lastly, we can say that through cohesion and commitment to maintaining a supportive and co-operative team ethos, team members can defeat a bully, even an influential bully like a potential major new customer. The sales team demonstrates that defeating a bully does not require that the team members decide in advance how to work together in the moment of an attack. It simply requires that each person makes an individual, firm commitment not to remain passive in the face of bullying behaviour, but instead to apply simple but effective principles in the moment of attack, and keep applying them until the incident is over.

Key Principles for Defeating Team Bullying

Let's recap the important points from this chapter by distilling the key principles you need should you be unfortunate enough to become the target of a team bully. Each of these principles is optimally employed at the moment of an attack, not afterwards. We will illustrate each principle with a short example. In each example, the team bully has already commenced their campaign, and the target is well aware of the situation they are facing. In some of the examples, the target confronts the bullying behaviour, in others it is a member of the target's team who does the confronting.

Key Principle One: Create Consequences for the Bully to Deal With

Team bullies want to make you, the person they are targeting, 'the problem' and will use a variety of tactics to place you in that position. These tactics can include highlighting your supposed deficiencies and failings; commenting on your mistakes and errors of judgement; remarking on any number of supposed character flaws or personal failings which they want to draw attention to; or, as in the above case study, threatening you. Their aim is to intimidate you and put you onto the back foot. Creating consequences for the bully to deal with means putting the issues back to the bully. It involves *placing the spotlight on them and their conduct* and requires them to give account for their behaviour.

An example is the situation where a bully delivers critical feedback to their target in front of their team colleagues. The feedback is subtly undermining, couched in terms that are demeaning and belittling. The target is embarrassed and ashamed at being spoken to like that in front of his colleagues, but nonetheless he is unwilling to remain silent and passive. He regains his composure, holds his head high, and in a respectful but firm tone says: 'I value feedback because it enables me to learn. The issue I am concerned about here is your tone. If you were to give me that feedback again, this time worded so that it is obviously designed to help me improve, how you would re-phrase it?' Now it is the bully who is in the spotlight, feeling embarrassed and uncomfortable.

Key Principle Two: Use Your Personal Power Wisely in the Moment of an Attack

Even in the moment of an attack by a powerful or influential foe, you have sufficient personal power available to you to prevent the bully having it all their own way. Personal power is your right to decide for yourself what you will say and do, what you believe (especially about yourself), how you will behave, and what values you will work and live by. No matter how limited they may be in some circumstances, you will have some choices available to you in the moment of an attack. Making a wise choice and acting on it is an effective way of mitigating distress and confusion. It may not decisively alter the character of the bullying dynamic which the bully is trying to create for that campaign, but it can prevent you from feeling overwhelmed by that incident.

An example is the situation in which a team bully fabricates a series of lies about the quality of the work recently completed by their target, repeating those lies at a team meeting in front of her. The target is so floored by the assault that she is shocked into silence. She knows full well that what has been said about her is completely untrue, but she is sufficiently stunned that she cannot find anything to say in response. In the silence which follows the slanderous description of her work, one member of the team shifts slightly in his chair, makes eye contact with the bully and says in a factual but low-key tone: 'I don't believe everything you say.' Now it is the bully's turn to feel uncomfortable. The bully is faced with the task of justifying what he has said, retracting it or doing neither, none of which changes the fact that the courageous team member has put the truth – that the bully is an unreliable witness – onto the table, and everyone else in the team has heard it.

Key Principle Three: Use the Facts to Confront Team Bullying

Bullies who distort the truth, misrepresent the facts or are subtly or blatantly dishonest run the risk of being unmasked by the truth. Truth always trumps lies, and when truth is put onto the table in the moment of an attack it alters the evolving bullying dynamic, sometimes stopping it dead. The truth includes your feelings of shock and surprise at being misrepresented, as well as the verifiable proof and sources of evidence available to you. In circumstances where a bully is lying, slandering or otherwise mispresenting you, there will always be facts available to you that you can use to confront bullying behaviour.

An example is the situation where the bullying manager decides to escalate their campaign against their target, and arranges a meeting with him and his peers at which to present the view that the target is failing to reach his performance objectives on their joint project. The target is an unassuming and understated character, who has always had exemplary feedback from previous managers. The bullying manager wants to attack him in front of his two peers to add to his embarrassment and shame, and to find out how susceptible to collusion these two more robust colleagues may be. The 'feedback' takes the form of criticism only, and is delivered in a robust and vigorous fashion, ignoring all the positive and praiseworthy aspects of the target's work. The bullying manager's opinion that the target's performance is below par is presented as a fact. Throughout the entire 'feedback' the bullying manager talks over the target, denying him the right to defend his performance, and dominating and interrupting him whenever he tries to speak. The shocked target is faced with the task of deciding how to handle the fact that his competent and effective performance – although delivered low-key and under-stated in style – has been characterised by his manager as well below par in an aggressive and destructive confrontation. He also has to decide what to say to his two colleagues, both of whom are silent witnesses to his ordeal, and who remain in the room with him. In the silence which follows the attack, he tells the meeting that he does not recognise the picture of himself or his performance which has just been painted, that he is on schedule as far as his key performance indicators are concerned, that this is a matter of record and he can prove it, and that he would value the opportunity to sit down with them and go through the evidence. Now it is the bullying manager who must decide what he will do next. He is faced with a situation he was not expecting: a target who can marshal the facts and the truth to confront him and, potentially, expose him as a manager who allows his personal prejudices to colour his feedback to the extent that he bullies top performers.

Key Principle Four: Believe in Your Own Opinion and Verbalise It

Team bullies want to undermine your belief in yourself to such an extent that you start to doubt your own mind. A skilled bully wants to create a situation in which you experience such a level of self-doubt that you think twice before saying what you want to say, or don't say it at all for fear that whatever you say, you will be attacked again. The antidote to this situation this two-fold. Firstly, recognise bullying behaviour for what it is: a tactic designed to undermine you. Words spoken by a team bully are not the truth about you or your work. They are words designed to undermine your self-confidence, self-esteem and self-belief. Seen from this perspective, they need not puncture you or have the power to change what you think about yourself *because they are not true*. Secondly, you do not have to disbelieve your own opinion no matter how much the bully wants you to. Stand by your own views and perceptions. Verbalise what you think and give your point of view. Why? Because most team bullies will only use the room for manoeuvre you inadvertently give them. If you demonstrate that you can calmly and clearly give your point of view, even under provocation, many bullies will think twice about continuing to target you.

An example is the situation in which a bullying peer attacks her team colleague for messing up a key client account. The bullying peer provides details and 'facts' which support her case, presenting them all with a level of aggression and sarcasm which initially floors her target. Having taken a few moments to regain her poise, and injecting both feeling and certainty into her tone, the target says: 'I haven't done that. What are you talking about?' This statement of belief in her own opinion, coupled with a neat question calling the bully to account, changes the entire dynamic between them. Now it is the bully who is on the back foot, and who needs to justify their false allegations.

Key Principle Five: Using Powerful Body Language Builds Your Confidence

Team bullies have an instinct for vulnerability and are on the look-out for any non-verbal signals you may give that you are on the back foot, lacking confidence or experiencing self-doubt. Using confident body language, even when you might not feel confident, is a powerfully self-preserving thing to do. It not only impacts the bully but it also helps to build your own self-belief. Powerful body language consists of keeping your shoulders back, holding your head high, maintaining level eye contact, sitting forward with your hands on the table if you are at a meeting or standing with your torso held upright and your feet planted firmly on the ground. Presenting yourself like this whenever you meet the bully will work in your favour. It may dissuade the bully from making an attack, will ensure that any rejoinders you make to bullying remarks come across as confident and unequivocal, and will prevent you from softening or undermining an otherwise effective rejoinder with non-verbal signal that you are uncomfortable or uneasy.

An example would be the situation in which the bully attacks his target for sitting passively and failing to contribute at a meeting. The target rebukes the bully with the words: 'I am considering what is being said and will speak when I am ready.' As she says these words, she wrings her hands, breaks eye contact with the bully and sits back in her chair. The bully notes her discomfort and attacks her again a few moments later. Consider the difference in the impact of her words on both her own self-confidence and on the bully, should she have used powerful body language instead. In that case, the target would have said exactly the same words but she would have held her head high, placed her hands firmly on the table, shifted slightly in her seat preparatory to speaking, and maintained level eye contact with the bully as she spoke. The bully would have noted her composure under attack, her poise in rebuking him and her confidence. He would have been highly unlikely to attack her again during that meeting.

It is vital that you learn to use powerful body language, practising it every day in the mirror, until you can carry yourself confidently as a matter of course. The act of making even one powerful confrontation can give your self-belief and self-confidence a huge boost as you realise that you are not powerless or helpless in the moment of an attack, and can more than hold your own.

In each of the following chapters, you will read longer case studies and shorter examples in which the target makes effective rejoinders to bullying remarks. In each of these scenarios, you can assume that the target uses confident body language during their rebuke to the bully.

Summary of Key Points from the Chapter

The team bully wants to create a bullying dynamic simultaneously with you, their target, and with the wider team. The team bullying dynamic consists of two interconnected strands. Firstly, the bully's use of behaviour which is designed to intimidate you, keep you on the back foot and keep them in charge of encounters between you. Secondly, the bully's desire to create altered power dynamics within the wider team in which established allegiances shift, and different team members are faced with a decision about whether to confront the bullying and support you, remain 'neutral' or collude with the bully.

A skilled team bully will conduct their campaign to set up dynamics in which you feel isolated, coerced and alone, your team colleagues feel afraid, anxious and conflicted, and everyone in the team loses power and influence as relationships alter and connections fray. If you are particularly unfortunate, you could end up feeling that the bully holds all the cards, you have no support, you have to comply with the bully's will, and that these dynamics are set in stone.

The good news is that these dynamics are not set in stone, even if that feels true to you. You and your team colleagues have a lot more influence that you realise and, used wisely, you and your team colleagues can interrupt, alter or prevent the bullying dynamic. What you say and do, and what your team colleagues say and do, at the time of an attack does influence the way that the team bullying dynamic evolves from that moment onwards. Depending on what they say at the time of attack, your team colleagues can mitigate the impact of an assault by affirming you as a person, and as a valued co-worker. This is true even if the bully has more organisational authority than any of you.

A key set of skills is learning to utilise the four principles for handling team bullying effectively in the moment of an attack. These principles could be used just as effectively by you, the target, or by any of your team colleagues who are witness to an attack.

The first of these principles is to create consequences for the bully to deal with such that the spotlight is removed from you, the target, and placed on them. This action means that they become the one who has to account for their actions, justify themselves and feel the discomfort of being under scrutiny.

The second principle is to use your personal power wisely to iden-tify and utilise the choices available to you, be they behavioural or verbal options. In certain circumstances, the choices available to you may be limited, but there will always be something that you can say or do which sends back a clear message to the bully that, however much pressure they put you under, *you* are still in charge of you, at least to some extent.

The third principle is to use the facts to confront the falsehoods, lies and slanders of a team bully. Whenever a bully employs these methods, the facts will unmask them. Your job is to find the courage to put the facts on the table knowing that in most cases these truths will prove decisive in that encounter. In some circumstances, they will prove decisive enough to stop the entire campaign.

The fourth principle is to believe in your own opinion and verbalise it during an attack. Bullies want you to doubt yourself to such an extent that you can't easily say what you mean, or verbalise your opinions at all. Recognising that their bullying tactics are designed to undermine you limits the effectiveness of these strategies, and makes it possible for you to speak up. Standing up for yourself and speaking up mitigates against the considerable distress you might otherwise feel after the incident. Just as importantly, it tells the bully that you know your own mind, are not incapacitated by their bullying (although you may *feel* vulnerable), and are fully able to put your view on the table to confront them. Under these circumstances, many bullies will desist.

The fifth principle is to use powerful body language, practising it every day until you can carry yourself in a confident manner even if you don't feel confident. Confident body language not only impacts the bully, dissuading them from continuing to target you, it also enhances your own self-confidence and self-belief. Confident body language also prevents you from undermining an otherwise effective rejoinder to a bullying comment by disguising your discomfort or self-doubt. Powerful body language involves you holding your head high, maintaining level eye contact with the bully, standing with your feet planted firmly on the ground or sitting forward at the table, and keeping your shoulders back.

Questions for You to Consider

In this chapter, we have been examining the team bullying dynamic which the bully wants to create, and the principles and skills which will enable you and your colleagues to respond effectively in the moment of an attack. You may now want to apply this material to your own experience by responding to the following questions. You can jot down your answer to each in the space below it.

Call to mind a specific incident in which you were subject to attack, in which at least one of your colleagues was present as a witness.

1. What happened during the attack? How did you react at the time?

2. Which of your team colleagues was witness to the attack? How did they react?

3. What did you say or do which interrupted or altered the team bullying dynamic that the bully was trying to create?

4. In what ways did the interventions of your team colleague(s) interrupt or alter the team bullying dynamic?

5. To what extent did you or your team colleague(s) create consequences for the bully to deal with?

6. To what extent did you or your team colleague(s) use your personal power to make a clear choice at the time of the attack?

7. To what extent did you or your team colleague(s) use the facts to confront the bullying behaviour?

8. To what extent did you or your team colleague(s) believe in your own opinion and verbalise it?

9. Looking back on it now, what else could you or your team colleague(s) have said or done that would have altered the character of the evolving team bullying dynamic?

Next Chapter

Chapter 6 explores the issues involved in handling team bullying when the bully is your manager. The chapter explores the circumstances in which a manager abuses their position, using their authority as a pretext to undermine their own team members. It illustrates how to handle a bullying boss in the moment of an attack, and explores how the actions of one confident team member can mitigate the impact of attacks on colleagues, enabling the team to function albeit under duress. The chapter focuses on the issues created when a manager routinely employs an unusual degree of aggression and rage with everyone in the team.

Chapter 6
When the Bully is Your Team Manager

Abuse of Formal Authority

The very fact that your manager uses bullying behaviour demonstrates that they have an under-developed, immature view of leadership, one that involves them abusing the formal authority they have been invested with by your joint employer. No matter what their level in the organisational hierarchy, your bullying manager likely regards their organisational authority as a badge of superiority, and uses their position and influence as the head of the team to coerce and browbeat you and your team colleagues. They probably enjoy the bogus sense of supremacy which their position affords them, and gain a spurious sense of power from coercing you and your colleagues, requiring you to do their will, at least to some extent. They are likely to be at their most self-satisfied when they have taken actions which reinforce their control over you and your colleagues. All of these traits coalesce to create a leader who, whatever their level of organisational authority, creates anxiety and distress among team members, damages their team's ability to perform, and fails to manage their responsibilities in a way which places serving customers at the top of their priority list. However, before we explore the modus operandi of a bullying manager in greater detail, let's take a sideways step to examine the characteristics of an effective team manager.

An effective team manager regards their authority as a responsibility which they need to discharge in the best interests of their organisation, their team and its customers. This means that they use the influence available to them to improve the quality of the products and services their team delivers. Effective managers see their job as primarily being to equip their team members with the tools, skills and know-how they need to perform optimally. They make it a priority to ensure that their team members have the levels of support they need to perform their roles effectively, including receiving timely and skilful feedback to enable them to do things differently and better.

Effective team managers are unafraid to give developmental feedback when required, pointing out areas in which team members need to make improvements, while balancing that critique with feedback about the positive and praiseworthy aspects of their team members' performance. An effective team manager understands the strengths and limitations of each member of their team, coaches specific team members as and when needed, and is available to give input and advice when asked. Their approach to building working relationships with their team is free from favouritism, is characterised by a degree of objectivity, provides calm leadership under stress, and encourages open and productive dialogue with each member of the team, as well as between team members. In short, the personal qualities of the effective manager play a significant role in their leadership. A mature and authentic manager builds enduring and robust connections with their team members, and wants to bring the best out of each of them so that the team can be as productive as possible.

With that in mind, let's now return to our description of a bullying manager. A bullying manager wants to use their organisational authority to dominate you and your team colleagues. Rather than use the influence available to them to improve team processes, the bullying manager approaches their interactions with you from the perspective of wanting to have 'power over' you. Their immature approach to leadership means that they want to retain control whenever they can, making a series of self-serving decisions which may have little to do with improving the work processes of the team, or enhancing the outcomes which the team produces. Instead, a bullying team manager takes every opportunity to belittle and demean you and their other targets, giving you the repeated message that *they* are in charge and that they require you to be subservient to their will. Bullying team managers may talk about their desire for top performance, but their behaviour creates high levels of anxiety, uncertainty and distress, making it hard for you and your colleagues to concentrate on your tasks or produce your best work. A bullying team manager's behaviour is likely to be the main reason that the work outputs of your team fall below par, however intermittently or consistently this occurs.

Altered Power Dynamics, Shifting Alliances

A bullying manager wants to create an atmosphere of heightened tension and anxiety in the team such that they can manipulate and alter established alliances, undermine workplace friendships and unhinge effective working relationships. Their aim in altering the bonds between team members in this way is to retain as much control over the members of the team as possible. Different bullying managers will have their own preferred methods of creating fractures and fissures in existing team relationships, each using methods which suit their personality and temperament.

Consider the following characteristics of bullying team managers:

- *They use their authority to belittle and undermine selected targets or the entire team.* A skilled bullying manager will subjugate their entire team, or selected targets, using a combination of coercive behaviour, aggression and threats. These tactics ensure that the manager's 'authority' is never questioned and that they remain in obvious charge of each and every interaction with the team members they are targeting.

- *They demonstrate low levels of empathy and high levels of sensitivity towards perceived slights towards themselves.* At their worst, a bullying team manager is likely to be either oblivious to, or impervious to, the destructive consequences of their behaviour, while responding with aggressive self-justifications and stinging retorts to any perceived disapproval or slur aimed at themselves, however unintended. In these circumstances, they can round on their supposed critic with a desire to exact retribution. This characteristic comes from a combination of a fragile sense of self and assumptions about their supremacy which make for a brittle hyper-sensitive character who can react with surprising aggression should they perceive any slight to their leadership, authority or control.

- *They avoid true responsibility while claiming that they are the ones doing all the work.* A bullying team manager can simultaneously demonstrate a pronounced ability to avoid self-reflection, to avoid taking responsibility for their destructive behaviour and to resist being held accountable for their poor managerial, decision-making and leadership skills. At the same time, they can berate individual team members, or the entire team, for not pulling their weight and leaving them with all the work.

- *They can be skilled at managing upwards.* A bullying team manager is likely to be skilled at manipulating the perceptions of the senior team to which they report. This skill-set enables them to present themselves to these senior colleagues as the one person in their team who is working hard, the one person who is holding it all together, and the main reason that the team produces effective outputs.

- *They coerce non-targeted team members into silent passivity.* A skilled bullying team manager will select the most effective deterrent from their preferred arsenal of tactics to ensure that members of the team remain passive and silent when they witness bullying attacks. These deterrents include setting up one-to-one meetings at which to intimidate team members who are not direct targets, bullying a target in front of them to send the message that they could be targeted next if they step out of line, threatening to expose their 'under-performance' to more senior managers, or using organisationally derived sanctions to pressure them into silence.

- *They use their authority to make self-serving decisions.* A bullying team manager will put their own feelings first when making decisions about the team's direction, work outputs or processes. Their need to be 'in charge' and to be 'in control' will take precedence over any other consideration, and can result in a series of decisions which do not support effective team performance, and which may even undermine it.

Controlling the Team

The bullying team manager's main aim in using bullying methods is two-fold. Firstly, they want to remove power from their targets, retaining that control for themselves, while secondly, they *want to control the actions of the entire team*. Even though they may only target specific people in the team, rather than everyone, their aim is to *extend the threat of attack to every member of the team* and so control the entire team dynamic.

Consider the following short example:

- A bullying team manager subjects two members of her team of six to intermittent bullying for a period of three weeks. Each of these two unfortunate members of the team is attacked in private and in public in front of the other members of the team. Such is the menace that the bullying team manager generates, and such is the confusion created by her intermittent attacks, that none of the members of the team confronts her. At the start of a particularly busy week, the bullying team manager decides to attack a member of her team who, up until that point, she has resisted the temptation to target. She sets up a team meeting at which to discuss upcoming work priorities, and at which to allocate specific tasks to each member of the team. When her team of six people is assembled, she turns towards her new target and, in a snide and cutting tone, tells her that she expects her to be more enthusiastic about taking on new and stretching work assignments. The new target is confused by this comment as she cannot remember having been offered a new and stretching work assignment, or turning one down. Aware that her colleagues are sitting silently and still, with their heads down and eyes on the meeting room table, she struggles to find something to say. In the silence that follows her bullying manager's initial remark, the new target spirals into confusion and becomes momentarily mute. Her manager senses her discomfort and attacks again. While looking straight at the new target she says in a slow malicious tone that she is uncomfortable with the attitude of several people in the team and expects more from them. For the remainder of the meeting, the new target is so distressed that she does not listen effectively to what her manager says, and leaves the meeting without a clear idea about what work she has been allocated. Most of the other members of the team remain quiet throughout the meeting, only speaking when spoken to directly by their manager. The way is now clear for the bullying manager to attack her new target for being 'work shy' or 'uncommitted' or 'irresponsible' should she fail to deliver to standard or on time, and for her to attack anyone else in the team whom she wishes to subjugate.

In this example, a skilled bullying manager subjects her targets to snide, cutting and demeaning comments, sometimes delivered in one-to-one meetings, and sometimes delivered in front of witnesses. The members of the team who have not yet been directly targeted are fully aware of the bullying methods of their manager, having witnessed her methods on many occasions. Team members who are not direct targets of her bullying feel considerable sympathy with the targets, but do not want to confront their manager for fear that she will also target them. The bullying team manager decides to extend her campaign to include a new target, and sets up a meeting at which to attack her. On the face of it, the meeting is a legitimate one. Its purpose is to discuss work priorities and allocate tasks for the coming week. However, the meeting is also an ideal setting for the bullying manager to reinforce her power over her team members by commencing a campaign against her new target while simultaneously sending the other members of the team the message that they could also be attacked. She strikes as soon as the meeting has assembled, making a vicious and unfounded attack on the hapless new target. Her words are unclear and confusing. They raise an issue about her performance and attitude without being clear what the issue is. The bullying manager communicates to the new target that she expects her to be more enthusiastic about taking on new and stretching work assignments. The new target has no idea what this means, as she cannot remember ever having been asked to take on a new and stretching work assignment. Nor can she remember turning one down. She is aware that her colleagues are all looking at the table, remaining passive and distant from her distress. As she tries to recover from the first snide attack, she is subject to a second incident of bullying straightaway. This time, her manager shifts the emphasis of her attack to unspecified members of the wider team, but remains steadfastly looking at the new target as she speaks. This way of behaving makes it clear that, even though she is looking at one person only, she is including unnamed other people in the room in her bullying observation. In an openly malicious tone, she says that she is uncomfortable with the attitude of several people in the team and expects more from them. She deliberately does not specify exactly which members of the team she is referring to, a ploy which puts the question into everyone's mind, including the new target, that she may be referring to *them*. Now every member of the team feels acute anxiety. They have no clear idea what she is referring to, so they do not know what to do to address the situation. All of them experience a jolt in their stomach as their energy goes inwards to cope with the escalating threat of bullying. Each of them becomes isolated in their own personal nightmare as they consider the possibility that their bullying manager may target them. They now know that they are all likely targets, but that none of them feels equipped to speak up and confront the bully. Their manager has succeeded in striking fear into each of them individually, and setting up a dynamic in which none of them supports anyone else, leaving each of them feeling isolated and alone.

The Difference Between Unjust Bullying Criticism and Developmental Critique

One of the main tactics available to a skilled bullying manager is to take advantage of their role by making an unjust attack on your *performance*. Although they present their 'feedback' as legitimate comment on your performance, your bullying manager is unlikely to want to assist you to improve your performance. Rather, your bullying manager delivers the 'feedback' with the intention of undermining your self-belief and causing you to doubt yourself.

This tactic is particularly effective if you are a conscientious worker, someone whose self-esteem is linked, at least in part, to your performance. In this case, bullying feedback delivered as part of a campaign against you could result in your experiencing a severe dip in self-confidence and self-belief.

No one likes hearing that their performance is under-par, and some managers are more skilled than others at providing useful feedback. But the key issue we are discussing here is the *intention of your manager.* What are the signs to look out for which would indicate that the 'feedback' delivered by your manager is bullying criticism as opposed to developmental critique? For the purposes of making this distinction clearly, the contrast presented below is between bullying criticism and skilled developmental critique delivered by an able manager who gives effective, useful feedback.

Unjust Bullying Criticism	Skilled Developmental Critique
The tone of the feedback is personal and punitive: it sends you the message that you are at fault or are not good enough	The tone of the feedback is objective and solutions-focused: it sends the message that there are issues with your work which need to be addressed
The feedback is confusing, unclear or bogus: you leave the meeting without a clear idea of what you have done wrong or what to do differently and better	The feedback is clear and issues-based: you leave the meeting with a firm idea about what you need to do differently and better, and the benefits to the team of you making these alterations
Your manager talks at you and doesn't listen to you: you find it difficult to interject, clarify what is being said, or ask questions	Your manager talks with you and listens to your point of view: you find it straightforward to discuss the issues, ask questions, or ask for clarification of points you don't understand
Your overriding impression is of your manager's desire to attack you by misrepresenting your supposed failings, exaggerating your supposed errors or making things up about you or your work that are not true	Your overriding impression is of your manager's desire to identify specific, defined aspects of your work which need attention, and to equip you with the knowledge and confidence to address them
You leave the meeting feeling confused, shamed or angry, and you may even feel a failure	You leave the meeting feeling sure about what you need to do differently and better, and able to make a start on these tasks even if you subsequently need more input

Let's see how these themes play out in a longer example.

Case Study 6: A Team in Crisis

The HR director of a major hotel chain has an enclosed office in the corner of a large open plan space in which the rest of his team work. The HR director is a lonely man. Never married, he lives on a large property outside town and rarely has visitors. A keen amateur cricketer, he keeps a cricket ball on his desk. At work, he routinely subjects all his office-based team to bullying behaviour characterised by an unusual degree of aggression. Volatile, without any discernible self-control, and likely to flip into a rage without warning, the HR director makes it his habit to arrive at his office at 10.30, leave for a two-hour lunch in the directors' dining room at 12 noon, and depart for home at 4.30 in the afternoon. Most of the HR team arrive at 9, with the assistant HR director arriving two hours' earlier at 7, and regularly working a twelve-hour day. The assistant HR director was recruited from a major conference provider two years previously. He is subject to the irascible outbursts of his boss along with everyone else. But, unlike them, he feels sorry for his boss rather than afraid of him, and makes it his business to protect his colleagues as much as possible from the unpredictable anger of their bullying manager. Much of the assistant HR director's time and energy is taken up with this task. He accompanies members of staff into their boss's office for meetings he does not otherwise need to attend. During these meetings, he challenges any unjust criticisms levelled at team members by their bullying boss and interjects should he feel that their manager is becoming unreasonably aggressive. The assistant director also provides direction, feedback and coaching to every member of the team in the stead of his boss, and it is he who takes it upon himself to have the most challenging conversations about the team's work with the HR director. The department operates in spite of the HR director, not because of him, and owes much of its success to the tenacity of the assistant HR director and the loyalty to him of the wider HR team. None of this is known to the board members who run the hotel chain. The HR director is pally with all the other directors, and uses his lunchtime meetings with them to cement his reputation in their eyes as firm but fair, effective and hard-working.

In the pressured run-up to the hotel chain's annual conference, the HR director is even more unpredictable than usual. He is aware that his team are struggling to manage their workload due to the fact that two members of his team have resigned in the previous week, and two more are off sick with stress-related illnesses. The HR director regards 'stress-related illness' as a short hand for idleness and is appalled that two of his team members should be so unprincipled as to take paid time off work on a pretext. He considers hiring a new female team member and steps outside his office to call the assistant HR director into his presence. He does this using the words: 'Where is my man?' The assistant HR director looks up, steps away from his desk and walks towards the HR director's office. As soon as he steps over the threshold the HR director yells at him 'What took you so long?' even though it has taken the assistant director a matter of a few seconds to enter his boss's office. Without waiting for an answer, the HR director walks behind his desk and sits down. Leaving the assistant director standing in front of him, the HR director says: 'What are you like with headstrong women?' The assistant director looks him in the eye and says: 'Just as good as with headstrong men.' The HR director immediately flies into a rage, picks up the cricket ball which he keeps on his desk, and hurls it in the direction of the assistant HR director. The assistant director sticks out a hand and neatly catches the ball just before it impacts his chest.

The HR director then leans back in his chair, steeples his finger tips and, in a tone of withering contempt, says to his assistant HR director: 'I am sick of the sight of you. Just get out!' The assistant HR director is used to his boss's intolerant and unreasonable outbursts. He takes a few seconds to compose himself, during which time he maintains level eye contact with his boss. He then replaces the cricket ball onto the desk before walking in a measured tread out of the room.

Later that day, the HR director calls the newest female member of the team into his office. The assistant HR director hears her being summoned, and decides to accompany her. During the short meeting which follows, the HR director turns snide, personally offensive and sarcastic as he characterises the female team member's work as 'sloppy', 'uninspiring' and 'dull.' The female member of staff is shocked at being spoken to like this. She knows she is a competent HR professional and, although having heard other people talk about him, has not had personal experience of her boss's malign aggression before.

Unable to handle being spoken to in such a vitriolic way, she angrily tells him to substantiate his unjust allegations. The HR director looks at her with withering contempt and, in an openly pitying tone of voice, tells her that if she wants to work in his team she will need to toughen up and take it on the chin. He then summarily dismisses them both with a disdainful wave of his hand and, turning back to his paperwork, waits for them to leave his office.

A Team in Crisis: Analysing the Team Dynamics

Let's examine the dynamics which play out between the HR director, the assistant HR director, the newest female team member and the wider HR team.

The HR director routinely uses a combination of verbal aggression, physical aggression and unpredictable rage-filled outbursts to control everyone in his team. At the same time, he is careful to manage his relationships with his fellow directors in such a way that they believe him to be effective in his role. He is unusual in that he displays no obvious self-control, has no empathy for anyone he attacks, and apparently no remorse about his actions. His behaviour is that of a man who enjoys throwing his weight around, intimidating his team members, taking his rage out on anyone he chooses whenever he chooses, and experiencing neither guilt nor shame about his actions. As a leader, he is disastrous. Quite apart from the terrible toll of distress, anxiety and fear which he randomly visits on his team members, he abrogates his responsibility to lead the department. He is present in his office for only a portion of each working day, routinely arriving late and leaving early, and spends each lunch time managing his relationships with his peer group. He leaves the day-to-day running of the department in the hands of the assistant HR director without either acknowledging this fact openly or taking it into account in his dealings with him. The HR director is a man who has an insatiable need for power over his team, and who demonstrates a degree of contempt for them which is alarming.

The assistant director is a conscientious and compassionate man. Less afraid of this boss than anyone else in the team, he is prepared to stand up to him in their one-to-one meetings. He also makes it his business to protect his colleagues, as much as possible, from the rages and outbursts to which their boss routinely subjects them. The assistant director works much harder than anyone else in the team. He uses his energy to cover for his boss's shortcomings by managing the team even though that role should fall to his boss. He regularly coaches his team colleagues, provides them with feedback, and clarifies their priorities for them. He works much longer hours than his boss or anyone else in the team, spending twelve hours a day in the office.

The rest of the staff are terrified of their boss's unpredictable and fiery temper. They cower at their desks, trying to get on with their work as best they can, hoping to avoid another encounter with their manager, and hoping to get home unscathed, at least on that day. Unsurprisingly, two members of the team have recently resigned, and two more are off work with stress-related illnesses. The HR director has no time for stress-related conditions. Completely blind to his own shortcomings, and demonstrating a jaw-dropping degree of insensitivity, he loathes the fact that they are prepared to take time off work on what he regards as a fabricated pretext. In the run-up to the annual conference, the HR team are struggling to keep up with their workload. The fact that the team is able to deliver on any of its targets, and that it keeps going at all, is largely due to the efforts of the assistant director and the dedication of a team which perseveres under extreme duress, partly out of loyalty to him.

This is a team in a permanent state of crisis. Most of the energy in the team goes towards coping with the HR director's appalling behaviour, his staggering levels of rage-fuelled aggression and his complete lack of respect for anyone in the team. Team members struggle to concentrate on their work on a daily basis, and are terrified that they may be subject to unpredictable physical and verbal assault. Unsurprisingly, some members of the team become ill and take time off work, and the team struggles to handle its workload. Apart from the courageous assistant director, none of them has successfully stood up to their boss.

At first glance, the HR director seems in an unassailable position. His place in the organisational hierarchy, his use of unusual levels of aggression, his lack of self-reflection and his callousness towards his staff make him a formidable foe. As HR Director he is the head of the management chain, and this makes it very difficult for any member of the team to make a complaint about him. Should any member of staff wish to make a complaint about another member of staff, it is the HR Director who would handle the complaints and investigation process. What can we learn about the HR Director that might provide us with some insight into his extreme behaviour?

The Psychological Profile of the HR Director

The HR director is a man consumed with two internal issues: his under-developed sense of self, and his explosive aggression. These two facts of his internal landscape are inextricably linked. The HR director's fragile sense of self means that he lacks a developed sense of identity or self-esteem. He is consequently woefully under-equipped with interpersonal, managerial or leadership skills. He covers up these deficiencies with an exaggerated reliance on what he regards as his authority, his status and his control over his team members. In practice, this means that he is unable to handle the pressure he feels when dealing with normal day-to-day interactions with his more socially skilled team members. He is particularly intolerant of any perceived failing, weakness or lack of application on the part of any of his staff, or towards any perceived slight by them towards himself. Under any of these circumstances, he can react with extreme aggression, belittling and demeaning his team members in a misguided attempt to re-establish his fragile internal equilibrium by puffing himself up in a false sense of his own importance.

The HR director's inner world is so shaky and friable that he is constantly in danger of exploding, even in circumstances where there is no objective threat to his fragile self-esteem. Under the slightest genuine pressure, such as the approaching annual conference or being short staffed, his inability to manage his own emotions becomes acute. Even holding a civil conversation with a member of his team is beyond him, and he resorts to levels of vicious aggression that are shocking in the workplace in an attempt to re-establish 'power over' the team member he is talking to.

When dealing with a team member who possesses greater self-esteem and a more securely developed identity than he does himself, the HR director is at an immediate and permanent disadvantage. To counteract his discomfort, he uses two tactics, both of which are designed to diminish his team members and assert his supremacy over them. With the assistant director, his first tactic is to refer to him as 'my man'. He doesn't call him by his name. Instead, he steps out of his office into the open plan area of the space, and shouts 'Where is my man?' His second tactic is to try to wrong-foot the assistant director by directing aggressive questions at him out of the blue. As soon as the assistant HR director enters his office, the director attacks him with the words: 'What took you so long?' even though the assistant HR director responded immediately to being summoned. Without waiting for an answer, the HR director follows that question up with another straightaway, asking his team member: 'What are you like with headstrong women?' This represents a second attempt to undermine the assistant director, this time suggesting that he might not be confident working with strong women. In truth, it is more likely to be the HR director who lacks the inner strength to work comfortably alongside a strong woman, but rather than own his shortcomings, he suggests that they pertain to the assistant HR director, a proposal he makes aggressively in the form of a question.

Before we return to examine the mind-set of the HR director in more detail, let's take a sideways step and explore the inner world of the assistant HR director.

The Psychological Profile of the Assistant HR Director

The assistant HR director is a compassionate and responsible man, someone who recognises the vicious nature of his boss and makes it his business to protect his team colleagues as much as possible. He has a well-developed sense of self. His sufficiently developed self-esteem means that he doesn't crumble under the verbal tirades generated by the HR director. Equally, he doesn't get obviously upset, feel angry with him or want to hide from him when the HR director becomes aggressive. Instead, he stands his ground and gives as good as he gets. When the HR director says: 'What are you like with headstrong women?' he looks his boss in the eye and says: 'Just as good as with headstrong men.' This is a clever response because it simultaneously tells the HR director that he is not thrown by the question, that he regards the HR director as a headstrong man, and that he isn't intimidated by him. The assistant director knows that by saying this he is protecting his inner self and pushing back on the challenging aggression being displayed by his boss. He also knows that, while he has given as good as he got, his boss is unlikely to back down.

Let's now return to our examination of the HR director to see how he responds to this composed and witty riposte.

More on the Psychological Profile of the HR Director

The HR director cannot cope with the self-possessed reply given to him by his assistant HR director *because it demonstrates that his more junior colleague is not prepared to submit to his, as he sees it, authority and superiority*. The HR director becomes instantly enraged. He picks up the cricket ball which he keeps on his desk. In a fit of rage, he hurls it at the assistant HR director, aiming for his chest. His attempted assault is thwarted by the assistant director, who fields the ball in a neat catch. The assistant director does not flinch during this incident. Neither does he give any outward sign of having been alarmed. The HR director observes his outward lack of fear, and again is faced with the failure of his power play. This time, he reacts by sitting back in his chair, steeples his finger tips and says in tones dripping with contempt: 'I am sick of the sight of you. Just get out!' He really does mean exactly that. He is sick of the sight of the assistant HR director *because he cannot find a way to puncture his self-esteem and gain control over him.* He has tried calling him 'my man', a patronising epithet at best. He has berated him for taking too long to arrive in his office when he entered it seconds after being summoned. He has tried asking him direct questions designed to unsettle him, including suggesting that he might have a problem working with strong women. He has tried throwing a cricket ball at him. None of these ploys has succeeded in undermining the assistant HR director's calm and composed way of handling himself. None of them has resulted in him giving any of his power to the bullying manager he works for. Faced with such a level of inner confidence, the HR director is defeated. He dismisses his team member from his office with a contemptuous wave of the hand, but he does this because *he has no other option if he is to remain in charge of their interaction*. The assistant HR director takes a few moments to compose himself, and then walks out of the room. In taking those few precious moments, he sends his bullying boss the message that he is leaving his office in his own time and at his own pace, and is still very much his own man. The moral victory is his, as he leaves the room without submitting to his grossly abusive manager.

On the face of it, the assistant HR director has plenty of grounds for making a complaint against his boss for bullying behaviour, either against himself or on behalf of his team, or both. He has witnessed and been subject to numerous incidents of team bullying, one of which involved a cricket ball being hurled at his chest; even given the fact that the HR director is pally with the other members of the board, why does he not take the bold step of making a complaint?

Firstly, even though the assistant director recognises the appalling nature of his boss's team bullying, he is also a compassionate man and feels sorry for him. He neither makes a complaint about him nor confronts him directly about his aggression, preferring to try and protect his team members as much as possible.

He recognises the deep loneliness in the life of his boss, but gives too much weight to his empathy and lets it cloud his judgement. He fails to hold his boss accountable *for creating his loneliness.* He fails to recognise that a man who is as misanthropic and irascible as his boss would find it hard to make or keep friends. He fails to realise that the HR director's loneliness is the inevitable outcome of his behaviour.

Secondly, he is well aware that any complaint would be a risky undertaking indeed. The HR director spends at least two hours a day with the other members of the board, a period of time in which he promotes the view that he is an effective and able leader. The assistant HR director knows full well that should he make a complaint, even about having a cricket ball hurled in his direction, he would have his hands full convincing anyone senior in the organisation that it was meant in anything other than jest. He is a senior HR professional and well aware that complaints of team bullying involve onerous, even gruelling, processes of interviews with everyone in the team, exhaustive searches for evidence, and result in much stress for everyone in the team. Quite apart from all these factors, who would he complain to? He would need to complain to a board member from outside HR, someone who wouldn't have the skills or knowledge to investigate in a fair or professional way. He is also concerned at the way in which his boss may react to any complaint, a reaction which would likely involve even greater levels of castigating and punishing behaviour. His decision not to complain, but instead to take every opportunity to demonstrate to the HR director that he alone decides what he feels, what he does and how he conducts himself is his victory against an egregious bully who routinely abuses his organisational authority and status.

A Team in Crisis: Conclusions

We have explored the psychological profiles of the two main protagonists in the case study. Let's now turn our attention to the other members of the team, and draw some conclusions about how they could handle their bullying boss more effectively. Their options are limited by the fact that he is the HR director and therefore the person whom they would approach should they wish to make a formal or informal complaint about the behaviour of a colleague. This doesn't preclude them from making a complaint to another member of the board, and they could do that jointly or individually, but it is a risky thing to do given how well he manages the perceptions of that group of people. We will concentrate on the behavioural options available to them.

Firstly, we can conclude that each member of the team needs to make a firm decision about when to draw the line, and what to do when it has been crossed. This threshold is personal to each member of the team. Each individual needs to make a conscious decision about what they are willing to tolerate, and what circumstances would be insupportable to them. The danger is that without such clarity, as the aggression used by the HR director escalates, they will adjust to it, let it go, keep their heads down, and continue to work for a man who is an atrocious boss. The more they allow him to subject them, individually and collectively, to his unchecked rages, the more likely it becomes that more of them will become ill with a stress related condition, need to take time off work, or simply lose so much confidence that they won't feel up to looking for another job. Each person needs to answer the question: 'What needs to happen for me to decide that it is time to resign?' and be prepared to keep that commitment to themselves.

Secondly, the members of the HR team need to find a way *to retain their composure and find something to say which demonstrates this to the HR director.* His aim is to control how they feel, to upset them and to keep them on the back foot in their interactions with him.

Finding ways to thwart this desire will preserve some or all of their self-esteem in that encounter. For instance, instead of getting angry when hearing her work described as 'sloppy', 'uninspiring' and 'dull', the female team member could put the spotlight back onto the bullying HR director. With her shoulders back and her head held high, she could say: 'That is not a definition of myself that I recognise. There is no one sloppy, uninspiring or dull in this room. As we both know, I am competent at what I do. That is why you hired me. Exactly what is the performance issue you are addressing here?' This combination of a series of factual statements and direct questions makes it clear that the female team member knows her own mind, is well aware of her competence, is not thrown by the personal attack from her bullying manager and is holding him accountable for what he said. She is challenging him. Furthermore, she makes a clear distinction between his destructive bullying criticism and true developmental feedback. She mustn't expect him to suddenly demonstrate a degree of managerial skill or even basic civility in response to this question. Indeed, he may throw her out of his office. But in asking that question in a calm and factual tone, she clearly demonstrates to him that his bullying has not resulted in her becoming upset. Indeed, she demonstrates that she knows how to take the spotlight off herself and place it onto him. In doing so, she will be making it plain to him that he can be as disrespectful, rude and aggressive as he wants, but that she, and she alone, decides what is true about her performance and what she feels. He does not.

Thirdly, we can conclude that the choice of the assistant HR director to protect his colleagues as much as possible, greatly contribute to the team being able to function and provide HR services to the hotel chain. The board are deeply indebted to him, but oblivious to this fact. Should the assistant director decide to leave, the HR department would likely collapse. The assistant HR director's personal support of each member of the team is also vital to their welfare. Each of them who enters their manager's office does so with the assistant director as a source of moral and practical support. Should the team member come under fire from their bullying manager, the presence of the assistant director as an active witness, a confident advocate and a supportive ear after the event will all go a long way towards mitigating the levels of overwhelm and distress which they might otherwise feel should they be left to handle an interaction with their boss alone. It is a very different experience to be bullied in a one-to-one meeting by a rage-filled boss than to be bullied by that same boss with a sympathetic and actively supportive person sitting alongside you. Although the presence of the assistant director will not change any of the words or actions of the HR director, *it can reduce the level of overwhelm that the target feels subsequently. They have someone to talk to, someone who witnessed what was said, someone who can subsequently talk it over with them, and help them process the experience.* However, even the active support of the assistant HR director cannot prevent some members of the team from becoming so depleted by their bullying boss's aggression that they understandably become ill.

Lastly, we can say that the HR team has a very tough time indeed in handling their explosive, rage-filled manager. He never completely succeeds in creating a team dynamic whereby every member of the team is isolated from the rest and completely in his power. He is unable to do this because of the actions of the assistant HR director, and because members of the team speak openly to one another about him in his absences. But he succeeds in subjugating many of them, at least to some extent, much of the time. He is a liability to his organisation and a formidable foe to the members of his team who choose to stay and work in his department.

Summary of Key Points from the Chapter

Your bullying team manager likely regards their organisational authority as a sign of their supremacy over you. A skilled bullying manager will take every opportunity to retaliate against you should they perceive that you are, as they see it, disrespecting their control over the team or their authority over you. In these circumstances, bullying managers who have an under-developed sense of self, or are insecure in their personal identity, may react with considerable aggression as they attempt to regain 'power over' you and re-assert their supremacy.

Bullying team managers want to achieve two things simultaneously during a campaign. Firstly, they want to remove as much power from you as possible, retaining that control for themselves. Secondly, they want to alter the established pattern of connections and relationships in the team, so that they can extend their control to every other member of the team.

Your bullying manager will employ a range of tactics designed to unsettle you and keep you off balance, reinforcing their assumptions about their authority over you. A bullying manager may be skilled at managing upwards, creating the false but persuasive impression to their own managers or board-level peer group that they are doing a great job.

By the very nature of their role, bullying managers have plenty of scope to target your performance, levelling unjust criticisms at you. They may be particularly motivated to do this if you are a conscientious person, someone whose self-esteem is at least partly predicated on you delivering excellent performance. There is a big difference between unjust bullying criticism and developmental feedback. Some non-bullying managers may not be that skilled at delivering developmental feedback, and may do so clumsily. But the key difference between unjust bullying criticism and developmental critique lies in the intentions of the manager. A bullying manager wants to deliver unclear, personal criticisms that are inexact and designed to undermine your self-esteem and self-confidence. A well-intentioned manager wants to deliver specific, issues-based critique from which you can learn, and which clarifies what you need to do differently and better.

Depending on the level of aggression they employ, and the persistence of that aggression, your bullying manager may be a very challenging foe indeed. Although your options may be limited at the time of an attack, your greatest ally is your ability to remain composed, putting the issues back to the bully, and demonstrating to them that they may be able to attack you but they cannot easily lie about you in your presence, misrepresent your work, or puncture your self-esteem.

In this chapter, we have been examining how to respond to an unusually aggressive rage-filled bullying manager. You may now want to apply this material to your own experience, even if your own manager is not as extreme a character as the HR director. You can jot down your answer to each of the following questions in the space below it.

Call to mind an incident in which you were subject to bullying by your team manager.

1. What happened during this incident? What bullying behaviours did your manager employ?

2. How did you handle this incident at the time?

3. To what extent did your manager provide you with bullying criticism (as opposed to developmental critique) during the incident? How did you respond to their unjust accusations?

4. In what ways were you able to demonstrate to your bullying manager that your self-esteem and self-confidence were not punctured by the assault?

5. Looking back on it now, what could you have said or done at the time which would have put the issues back to your bullying manager more effectively?

Next Chapter

Chapter 7 explores the issues involved in handling team bullying when the bully is your peer. The chapter explores how to handle the adversarial alliances that bullying peers want to create, and explores ways in which you can preserve your informal influence with team colleagues not directly involved in the campaign but who hear whispers about you. The chapter focuses on the issues created when two members of a peer group independently start to target the same colleague in team meetings, a situation to which everyone else in the group turns a blind eye.

Chapter 7
When the Bully is Your Peer

Effective Peer Relationships

Of all of your team relationships, those with your peers are the only ones in which there are no hierarchical power dynamics at play. Consequently, your peer relationships are likely to be the ones which operate mostly on the basis of informal influence and goodwill. Of course, in order to work with your peer on this basis you need to believe in their basic competence to do their job and their basic goodness as a person. But assuming that you do believe in both of these things, you aren't likely to instruct one another to undertake certain actions or perform certain tasks, because neither of you has formal authority over the other. Instead, you are likely to work together on the basis of mutual respect for your skills and abilities and, under normal working conditions, you will both work to keep the relationship viable. In an effective peer relationship, the esteem you have for one another as people, and your respect for each other's work, results in you working effectively together on smaller and larger tasks.

You may have closely structured working relationships or your roles may be inter-dependent, at least to some extent. You may need to make some joint decisions, collaborate effectively on certain tasks or solve some problems together. Your main task as peers is to find ways to get things done effectively on a regular basis so that the team can produce its goods and services to the required standard. However, it may be the case that you have differing levels of experience, knowledge or skills in certain areas of the team's work. At different times, each of you may defer to the other because you recognise your peer's greater expertise. You actively work together to keep the relationship practicable by expressing different opinions, resolving conflicts and getting things done productively. In a healthy team, it is often the quality of the connections that you have with your peer group that creates bonds of trust and belonging, and which enables you to enjoy the process of your work.

So, when one or more of your peers starts to bully you, the impact on you and your non-bullying colleagues can be significant. Before we explore the dynamics involved in peer bullying in some depth, let's return to the example from Chapter 1 of the skilled engineer who bullies three of his peers simultaneously. In that example, the bullying peer is intermittently 'nice' to his targets during his campaigns against them, a ploy which confuses them, putting doubt into their minds about whether or not he really is bullying them. The bully sees one of his targets sitting in his car in the company car park reading his emails, and decides to take advantage of the impromptu meeting. He approaches him, all smiles and bonhomie, gesturing to him to wind down the window. The target is thrown by the apparent good humour of a man who has been bullying him for the previous two weeks. He makes the mistake of lowering the window while remaining seated in his car. The bully chats for a few moments before using a cutting tone to tell him that he has better things to do than stand there talking to the likes of him. He then turns smartly on his heels, and walks away in a self-important manner. What could the target have done to protect himself from this attack?

Firstly, he needs to be on his guard as soon as he sees the bully approaching him. His recent experiences of the bully tell him that he is a man who is not to be trusted, a man who uses intermittent aggression and veiled hostility to attack him, and a man who now appears to be warm and friendly. The target needs to *trust his own experience and listen to his instincts about the bully* so he can avoid falling into the pitfall of self-doubt. His assessment of the bully's character is spot on. He *is* a duplicitous character. Acting in a friendly manner is a clear example of that duplicitousness. His warmth and friendliness does not mean that his basic nature has altered. It means that an attack is imminent.

Secondly, the target needs either to get out of the car so he can stand and speak with his bullying peer, or wind down the window and immediately say something which signals that he is on the front foot. What he mustn't do is stay in the car with his guard lowered. Getting out of the car alters the energy between him and the bully. It removes the power imbalance that is in play should he remain seated inside the car while his adversary remains standing outside the car. Winding down the window and immediately seizing control of the interaction demonstrates to the bully that the target is on guard. The target could say: 'I am in the middle of something. Can I get back to you?' or 'I need to make a call. What is it you want to talk about?' Neither of these openings is rude. Both are professional and work-oriented. But, critically, both retain him a measure of control and, depending on what the bully says next, enable him to end the interaction before it has got started, preventing an attack from taking place.

Lastly, the target needs to conduct this interaction, and every interaction with the bully thereafter, with a degree of controlled caution. He needs to adopt a tone which is polite, firm and professional, which makes it clear to the bully that he will speak with him but will do so only with his guard well and truly up. The combination of civility and professional guardedness will protect him should his peer suddenly try and bully him again *because he is expecting the attack, is prepared for it and therefore isn't likely to be thrown or punctured by it.* Under these circumstances, the impact of the attack will be muted or non-existent.

A Skilled Bullying Peer

An attack orchestrated against you by a bullying peer is different from an attack orchestrated against you by your manger due to the fact that they have no organisational authority over you. Consequently, a skilled bullying peer will often target you by trying to undermine your credibility and standing in the eyes of other team members, including your joint manager and any junior members of the team whom they can influence. A skilled bullying peer will work behind your back and during team meetings at which you are present to destabilise your reputation with other team colleagues, encouraging them to amend their positive view of you and replace it with a pejorative or harsh view of your competence, attitude or abilities. They will also attack you in one-to-one encounters. Cumulatively, the attacks can leave you feeling alone and isolated in team settings, and confused and sidelined in team meetings which you would otherwise experience, at least some degree, as being characterised by camaraderie and connection. When there are two or more bullying peers, each of whom is simultaneously orchestrating separate campaigns, the issues are compounded.

One of the challenges for the non-targeted peers is what to do in response to witnessing attacks against you. Each non-targeted peer has three options:

- *Passive enabling:* remaining passive and silent during the attack against you, absenting themselves from their responsibility to confront the bully.

- *Active collusion:* taking actions or saying things which actively support the bullying and add to the bullying dynamic you are faced with.

- *Effective confrontation:* challenging the bully at the time of an attack to combat the bullying and provide you with an ally.

Let's examine these three options as they relate to non-targeted peers witnessing an attack against you in a team meeting. The passages which follow describe why a non-targeted peer might adopt the role of passive enabler or active colluder, as well as illustrating how they might confront a bullying peer effectively. It is important to note that, while the power dynamics may be different, the following principles are also applicable when the witnessed attack is carried out by your manager or by a junior member of the team.

False Assurance: The Pitfall of Passive Enabling

Those of your peers who remain inactive, silent and still when they witness an attack against you adopt the stance of passively enabling the bullying. Their bystander apathy enables the bullying to continue *because their apparent indifference to the attack encourages the bully.* The bully learns that none of the peers who witnesses the attack is prepared to challenge them, confront them, create consequences for them to deal with or otherwise support you, the target. To a bully who is on the look-out for ways in which to wrest power from you, and from as many of your peer group as possible, these are powerful motivators to continue with an attack. Under these circumstances, the passive enablers in the team give some or all of their personal power to the bully, making it easy for them to continue with that attack and, if they wish, to attack again in subsequent team meetings.

The complication is that some of your peers who remain silent during an attack might not want to. They remain silent either because they are afraid of reprisals, or because they don't know what to say to confront the bully safely. These peers may be horrified at the attack against you but may simply lack the know-how to do anything decisive about it. However, other peers again may want to remain silent. They may keep their heads down, waiting for the attack to stop. These peers are unwilling to involve themselves in the situation which is evolving around them, and are unconcerned about the impact of that situation on either you or the team dynamic.

As mentioned previously, I take the view that you, the target, are best placed to alter the bullying dynamic, and that the optimal time to do this is during the attack itself. However, there is no doubt that should one or more of your peers support you during an attack, the message sent back to the bully is doubly powerful. So, let's consider in more detail some of the reasons why your peers may not want to confront the bully when they witness you being targeted, opting instead for the role of passive enabler. We will also discuss some of the implications for your subsequent relationship with them should any of your peers decide to handle things this way. For the purposes of illustrating these dynamics, we will assume that you are attacked by a bullying peer in a meeting attended by you and members of your peer group only:

- Some of your peers don't want to turn a blind eye to the attack, but end up doing exactly that, because they don't know what to say to support you or confront the bullying effectively. They remain silent during the attack, avoiding eye contact with either you or the bully, or both of you. Once the bullying ceases and the meeting moves on to its work topics, these peers involve themselves with the work agenda of the meeting, but fail to rebuke the bully or acknowledge that bullying took place. After the meeting, these peers can feel very uncomfortable indeed that they haven't spoken out against the bullying. Their shame and disappointment with themselves can result in them behaving differently around you from that point onwards. You may be tempted to take their altered behaviour to heart, reading it as a sign that these peers have abandoned you. This can be a very painful conclusion to come to, especially if you had enjoyed a fruitful or close working relationship with some or all of them. In some cases, their altered behaviour may indicate that they *have* taken a step away from you. But more often, their altered behaviour is their way of handling their own complicated feelings about their failure to support you when you were subject to attack, rather than an overt attempt to shun you. This distinction doesn't alter the fact that these peers do distance themselves from you, but it may help to lessen some of the distress associated with their decision.

- Other peers may be unwilling to speak out against the bullying for a different reason. Their reason is fear. They fear that if they confront the bully they will inevitably set themselves up to be targeted alongside you in that meeting, or subsequently. This group of peers believe that the act of confronting the bully will inevitably work against them, and that it would be a foolhardy thing to do. On the face of it, this may be a reasonable fear to have. But, in fact, the opposite is more likely to be true if they mount an effective confrontation in the moment of the attack. A bullying peer who has attempted to target you in front of one or more of your peers is *unlikely* to target the courageous peer who speaks out effectively against the bullying. In this case, the bully who has been effectively confronted will learn that *that* peer will not be a straightforward peer to target, and is therefore *unlikely* attack them in that meeting, groom them subsequently or pursue a campaign against them.

- A third group of your peers take the view that the bullying is a private matter between you, the target, and the bully, and that it does not concern them. This group of peers do not involve themselves in the incident because they are waiting for it to conclude so that the business of the meeting can resume. These peers misunderstand the nature of the interaction between you and the bully. They regard it as a continuation of a dispute between the two of you, or a conflict that has become personal, or a personality clash. They fail to see it for what it is: one peer trying to undermine the reputation, influence and credibility of another in front of some or all of their peer group, in the hope of removing power from as many of them as possible.

In any or all of these scenarios, your passive peer is making an error of judgement. Remaining on the side lines, no matter what the reason behind it, is a risky choice to make. It will not protect your peer from future attack should the bully be minded to target them and, in many cases, it compounds the degree of power that the bully wrests from their peer group during the attack. It is not a wise or self-protective path to take as it leaves the entire team vulnerable to losing increasing levels of power to the bully.

Active Collusion: A Misguided Strategy for Self-Protection

A minority of your colleagues may be tempted to join in the bullying, actively colluding with the bully against you. Their involvement in the bullying can be especially painful for you to handle. These peers may laugh or nod during the attack to convey support for the bullying. They may say things which actively endorse the attack, or they may extend it by making bullying comments of their own. In either of these cases, your actively colluding peer sides with the bully against you, something which can result in you feeling threatened and intimidated, especially if your other peers attempt to distance themselves from the incident by passively enabling it. Why might a peer choose to actively endorse the bullying you are subject to in this way?

The actively collusive peer takes the path of siding with the person they consider to be the 'strongest' in the meeting. They hope that by allying with the bully, they will preclude themselves from being targeted at that meeting or in the future. Some peers may decide to actively collude after witnessing the start of an attack against you in which everyone else in the room remains passive and uninvolved. The colluding peer dreads the prospect of being placed in a similar position. They dread the combination of distress, powerlessness and humiliation they would feel should they also be targeted in front of peers who do nothing to assist them. Their dread coalesces into a powerful motivator to collude in a misguided attempt to protect themselves. However, the choice to participate in the bullying will not prevent them from being targeted in the future. Nor will it even lessen the likelihood that they may be targeted in the future. Allying with an unprincipled and ruthless bullying peer is not a wise choice to make, and could back fire in any number of ways.

Let's explore some of the ways in which making this choice could work against your actively collusive peer in the long run. Once again, for the purposes of illustrating the dynamics, we will assume that you are attacked by a bullying peer in a meeting attended by you and members of your peer group only:

- *By joining forces with them, your collusive peer implicitly gives some or all of their power to the bully.* Given your collusive peer's primary desire for self-protection, their decision to join the bully may seem to them to be a good option to take. But it is a risky choice to make because of the signals it sends to the bully. Your collusive peer's active endorsement of the attack may take the bully by surprise or they may take it in their stride. But, either way, the bully will recognise that the colluding peer wants to join forces with them in *a manoeuvre designed to purchase their safety.* But the bully hasn't agreed to this outcome and may not want to unite with the colluding peer for very long, or at all. The bully will recognise that the *colluding peer wants something in return for their complicity, and this fact gives them power over their new ally.*

- *Far from securing their personal safety, the colluding peer has paved the way for the bully to attack them.* Bullies are on the look-out for signs of vulnerability which they can exploit. Your colluding peer has sent a very clear signal to the bully that they are so frightened of the prospect of attack, that they are willing to form an alliance with them in the hope of avoiding it. The way is now open for the bully to attack the foolish peer should they be minded to.

- *Rather than secure their own safety, by joining in the bullying the colluding peer has lost their integrity in front of their entire peer group.* All their peers witness their collusive bullying. They all witness the choice to ally with the bully in the moment of an attack. Every one of these relationships will alter from that moment onwards in larger and smaller ways, as the rest of the peer group recognise the venality of the collusive peer's character.

- *The bullying peer's relationship with themselves alters.* In all likelihood, this peer did not conceive the original attack on you. They did not conspire with the bully prior to the meeting to jointly attack you. Indeed, they may never have had a thought to bully a colleague prior to the moment of colluding against you. Rather, in the split second they had to make up their mind about how to respond to the bullying they witnessed, the colluding peer decided to be in cahoots with the bully. The colluding peer now has to live with this decision, and with its consequences for their self-image and self-esteem. They now know that they are capable of bullying behaviour, of forming an elicit alliance with an unprincipled colleague, and their self-respect may suffer accordingly.

So, what are the alternatives to adopting the role of a passive bystander or an active colluder? Let's explore them now, again in the context of an attack on you carried out by a bullying peer at a meeting attended by you and members of your peer group only.

Effective Confrontation: Refusing to be Complicit in Peer Bullying

The alternative to either passive enabling or active collusion is to confront in an effective and carefully-crafted challenge which takes the spotlight off the target and places it firmly and squarely on to the bully. Each peer who takes the path of effective confrontation:

- Sends the bully the clear message that their bullying behaviour will not be tolerated in the team.

- Informs the bully that their aggression is unacceptable and needs to stop.

- Positions themselves as someone who knows how to defend both you, the target, and themselves, making it *unlikely* that the bully will target them outside the meeting.

- Demonstrates to the bully that you, the target, have allies in the room who are prepared to take a stand.

- Demonstrates to you that you are not alone, and have active support.

There are many things that your non-targeted peers could say to confront the bully. Here are some examples, followed by a commentary highlighting the key principles illustrated by the scenarios. As before, the following incidents all occur in a meeting attended solely by the bully, the target and a number of other non-targeted peers only:

- In an aggressive and cunning attack designed to set her up to fail, the bully says to their target: 'I think you should start to contribute something useful to this team by undertaking the next Month-End Report.' The bully knows that this report is produced by the team's boss, a Board-level manager, and that the target does not have the skills or knowledge to produce it. In the moments following this attack, the target looks stunned. She struggles to find anything to say in reply, and looks to the peer on her right for help. In a clear and factual tone, with just an edge of irritation to it, this peer says: 'Your aggression is out of step with the tone of this meeting. Perhaps you would like to re-phrase that remark and I will then respond to it?' Before the bully can respond, a second peer says: 'From where I'm sitting, your suggestion would expose the team. We all know that that report needs to be written by someone at Board level. What do you mean by that suggestion?'

- In a cynical attempt to undermine the self-esteem of his target, the bully turns to her in a tone full of contempt and says: 'You don't really deserve a place at this table, do you?' The target bridles, but does not respond verbally. One of her peers moves his chair noisily forward to get the attention of the meeting. As the bully looks up at him, he says: 'I just heard you say: "You don't deserve a seat at this table, do you?" What exactly does that mean?' Two other peers nod to show their support for the challenge, and the target says: 'I'd like an answer to that question as well.' Now it is the bully's turn to feel acute discomfort as he notices that everyone in the room is looking directly at him.

- Two weeks into a subtle campaign of scapegoating and innuendo behind her target's back, the bully changes tack and openly attacks in a meeting. She calls her a 'snotty-nosed do-gooder', a 'rudderless ship' and calls her management of her project into doubt with the words: 'Where exactly do you get the gall to lead from?' In the seconds which follow these words, speaking quietly and slowly, the first peer says: 'You have just given me a window into your true character. I did not like what I saw.' A second peer says: 'The purpose of this meeting is to discuss the current sales drive. I suggest that you restrict your comments to that topic.' A third peer says: 'I am astonished by that outburst. You have just attacked a peer for having under-developed leadership skills when, in fact, she is an able leader. What do you mean by that?'

In each of these scenarios, a number of the non-targeted peers refuse to remain passive and silent when their colleague is targeted. They also refuse to collude with the bully in a misguided attempt to secure their own safety. Instead, they confront the bully in a series of carefully crafted, effective confrontations. Their words change the momentum of each meeting, taking it away from the bully who, on each occasion, is left shame-faced and in the spotlight. On each occasion, the bully misjudges the meeting by expecting its participants to actively collude or passively enable their attack.

The carefully crafted confrontations are effective because they simultaneously:

- Draw the line.

- Call the bully to account.

- Put the issues back to the bully.

- Provide life-affirming support to the target.

- Are presented in a factual, low key but influential way.

Peers who do not have these principles to work from may not know what to say in support of the target, and could end up remaining silent even if they don't want to be. What makes these confrontations so effective?

- *All of them avoid the pitfalls of contesting or debating what the bully said.* However well-intentioned, strategies for combatting bullying which involve contesting what the bully said, refuting it or disagreeing with it often don't work. They actually strengthen the bully's hand because they invite discussion of the bullying remarks, providing the bully with additional airtime to expand on their bullying themes. These strategies do not place the spotlight on to the bully but inadvertently keep it where the bully wants it to be, on the target's supposed shortcomings and deficiencies.

- *None of the confrontations defends the target directly, although all of them have the impact of providing the target with immense support.* Instead, each of the confrontations holds the bully accountable for what they said, puts the issues back to them, and requires the bully to take responsibility for the non-sense they just placed on the table. This approach is hugely supportive to the target, something which is achieved without creating a situation where the confronting peer *has to take sides.* Their objectivity is intact, and they avoid the pitfall of patronising the target or making them appear weak by obviously defending them.

- *The peers who confront avoid the pitfall of revealing emotion which would render them vulnerable.* Bullies are skilled at playing emotion straight back to you, turning any wobble in your voice back onto you in a renewed attack. Each of these confrontations avoids this pitfall because the remarks that are made are *only about the bully* and do not reveal any fear or anxiety on the part of the peer who makes the challenge. Each of the peers who makes a challenge recognises that keeping the issues on the bully will defeat the bully because it removes from them the degree of control they think they need to exert over the meeting.

- *Each of these responses sends back the clear message to the bully that they are outmatched, outnumbered and losing.* In each scenario, only a few members of the team speak. But their words swing the mood of the meeting away from the bully in a decisive way. Even a skilled bully cannot win against a room which contains determined people looking straight at them, requiring them to justify what they just said.

- *Each of the confrontations preserves the power of the peer group and prevents the bully from wresting any of it away from them.* Their active involvement in confronting the bullying results in the non-targeted peers retaining their full power as individuals and as a group. Although some bullies will try again, they can be under no illusions about how tricky it will be for them to remove power from that group of peers in the future.

- *The peers who confront the bully bolster at least some of their otherwise silent colleagues, enabling them to find the courage to challenge the bullying too.* Part of the power of those who confront is in their ability to give courage to their peers. These emboldened peers may nod in agreement or maintain steady eye contact with the bully in a show of non-verbal support for the confrontation. Some of them are enabled to speak, verbalising an additional challenge to the bullying. A shocked target may also be able to verbalise a challenge after hearing words of effective confrontation delivered by one of her peers.

The combination of factors highlighted above makes for a series of mightily effective confrontations. Each of the carefully crafted challenges makes it clear to the bully that they will have a struggle on their hands to remove power from the peers in the room, that the mood of at least some of the peers in the meeting is against them, and that they cannot win on that occasion. With some bullies, responses like these will prove decisive and they will desist from their campaign from that moment onwards. Others will persevere and try again, but with the new knowledge that at least some members of their peer group are actively supporting the target and are more than a match for their bullying tactics.

We have been examining what happens when a peer targets you, and the various ways in which non-targeted peers can respond to the bullying. Let's examine how these issues play out in a longer and more complex example.

Case Study 7: Inimical Peers

A team of six senior underwriters work closely together for their employer, a large international specialist insurance firm. Due to the complex nature of the bespoke policies which the firm underwrites, the team of six peers consider the risks associated with each new policy separately as individuals before coming together to discuss their views in a weekly policy meeting on a Wednesday afternoon. The output of the meeting is a jointly agreed policy for each new underwriting risk which is usually related to international fleets of merchant vessels or fleets of commercial aeroplanes. The team reports to the head of underwriting. In the normal course of his work, the head of underwriting does not attend policy meetings. In order for any changes to be made to the work allocation of any member of the senior underwriting team, all of them need to agree to the change.

The senior underwriting team contains two male members, each of whom has a reputation for using aggressive and bullying behaviour. Poor at connecting with other people, these two male members of the team specialise in African and Mediterranean shipping respectively. The remaining members of the team are all female, one of whom is a conscientious and hard-working underwriter who specialises in European airlines.

One particularly busy Wednesday morning, the European airlines specialist decides to run an issue past her Mediterranean shipping peer. The issue is an important one for her to discuss with him as she wants to clarify a key point before finalising her recommendation for the meeting that afternoon. The European airlines specialist rings her male peer's desk phone and hears his voice message. She walks up the flight of stairs that separates her floor from his, and searches for him. Unable to locate him, she asks several of his colleagues where he might be. None of them can enlighten her and, disappointed, she returns to her desk. Her experience of the Mediterranean specialist is of a peer who regularly disappears for long periods of time, making it a challenge to get his input on issues which need his attention.

The European specialist is aware that she is not the only member of her peer group who struggles to get the Mediterranean specialist's input on a regular basis. At the policy meeting that afternoon, she suggests that as a team they consider a procedure for letting one another know where they are going to be on Wednesday mornings, so that outstanding issues can be finalised straightforwardly before the Wednesday afternoon team meeting. She fully expects any number of her peers to support her proposal. Although she does not look at him nor mention his name, as soon as she finishes speaking the Mediterranean specialist becomes irate. In a raised voice, he begins sneering at her, insulting her in a sustained sarcastic outburst. Amongst other things, he calls her a 'goody two-shoes' and a 'girl guide', uttering both epithets with a shocking degree of contempt.

The European airlines specialist is stunned at being attacked so openly and in such a nasty way by her peer in a team meeting. As the furious tirade continues with comments about her 'sticking her nose into other people's business', she looks sideways at the colleagues seated to her left and right. She is dismayed to notice that none of them engages with the increasingly personal invective being generated by the Mediterranean specialist. Each of the other members of the team remains head down, silent and still, absenting themselves from the bullying attack. Rather than remain helpless, listening to insults being hurled at her, the European airlines specialist decides to leave the meeting and return to her desk. It takes her several hours to regain her composure. In subsequent policy meetings, she chooses every word carefully to avoid igniting the Mediterranean specialist's mercurial temper.

The following week, during a routine meeting which the European airlines specialist misses due to annual leave, the Mediterranean specialist proposes that he take over a large area of her non-policy work. This includes the supervision of two of her four trainees and the production of her in-house training manual for new underwriters. None of the other members of the team challenges this proposal. None of them points out that they need to discuss the issues at a meeting at which the European airlines specialist is present before agreeing to the changes. The Mediterranean specialist gives no reasons as to why he wants to take over her work, and makes no criticism of her performance in relation to the supervision of trainees or the production of the in-house training manual. The meeting ratifies his recommendation but does not inform the European airlines specialist about it. She finds out from a confused trainee on her return to work.

The European airlines specialist is shocked at the aggression of her male peer behind her back. But she is even more upset, disappointed and confused by the apparent complicity of the rest of her team colleagues. Feeling increasingly isolated, she is dismayed when one of the other female members of the team says to her: 'You make me very uncomfortable in team meetings because you make the Mediterranean specialist angry'.

Shortly after being told that she is to blame for his aggression, the European airlines specialist sees the Mediterranean specialist stomping angrily towards her in a busy corridor. In full view of everyone in the corridor, he makes a series of loud, critical comments about one of her recent policy recommendations, his face contorted with sneering fury. He tells her that she hasn't thought about the implications of her 'flimsy recommendation', has left the firm open to 'unmitigated risk', and 'hasn't understood the complexity' of the policy. Unwilling to be drawn into a public quarrel which would bring the senior underwriting team into disrepute, the European airlines specialist invites her male peer to a private meeting to discuss the issues. He abruptly declines, storming off in anger.

Over the next week, the European airlines specialist becomes increasingly concerned about the behaviour of her other male peer. The African specialist starts to make a series of non-urgent but important decisions about work processes that directly affect her work on days when she is out of the office. He also introduces new underwriting software to the team without informing her, leaving her embarrassed in front of her trainees. He starts to spread misinformation about her supposed views, telling their joint boss that she is not enjoying her job, has had a major disagreement with the Mediterranean specialist in a corridor, and is a nuisance at team meetings. In meetings when she is present, he dismisses her carefully worded recommendations with vague remarks like: 'I don't know why, but I just don't like the sound of that.' On each occasion that he makes a comment like this, his view is accepted by the rest of the team without question. At one team meeting, the European airlines specialist highlights a significant risk which she wants the team to take into account on a new policy. The African specialist dismisses her concern with a wave of the hand and the words: 'I just don't think that matters'. Once more, the team accepts his lead without demure.

Over the next fortnight, the European airlines specialist becomes increasingly distressed by the passivity of her female team colleagues towards their aggressive male peers, and by the way the two male members of staff dismiss or attack her input in team meetings. Over a series of consecutive team meetings, as she endeavours to make a professional contribution to the meetings, they jointly attack her decision-making, her points of view and her input to debates. She becomes distressed at work, crying at home in the evenings and at weekends. Feeling increasingly powerless and self-doubting, she starts to worry that she is doing things that provoke her male colleagues to aggression even though she can never quite put her finger on what it is she might be doing wrong.

Inimical Peers: Analysing the Team Dynamics

Let's analyse the dynamics at play in this scenario, playing particular attention to the key incidents in the action. Initially, the discussion of each separate incident will focus on how the passivity of the non-targeted female team members, and collusion of the two male members, contributes to the complexity of the situation unfolding around the European airlines specialist. Then, the discussion will move on to examine ways in which the target could handle those dynamics optimally.

Key Incident One: Initial Grooming Attack

In this incident, the European airlines specialist is subject to an extended personal attack in the form of a vitriolic tirade. The tirade is hurled at her by one of her male peers, the Mediterranean shipping specialist, during a team meeting with her peers. The attack comes out of the blue, after she has made a sensible suggestion that the peers tell one another where they will be on Wednesday mornings. During the attack, none of her peers says or does anything to confront the bully, or to interrupt his flow. They all remain passive and uninvolved, letting the bully continue with his extensive bullying remarks unhindered. Rather than be subject to further attack, the European airlines specialist leaves the room.

This incident represents an instance of the Mediterranean specialist controlling the entire meeting by using egregious aggression. It also represents an incident of successful grooming. But, unusually, the bully is not successful in grooming the European airlines specialist who more than holds her own by removing herself from an abusive situation. *Instead, the bully successfully grooms the remaining members of the peer group.* During the attack, all non-targeted peers adopt the role of passive enablers of the bullying. Each of them outwardly absents themselves from involvement in the issues raised by the bully's outburst, a pattern which continues during every other occasion that the European airlines specialist is attacked by either of her bullying male peers in front of her team colleagues. The message which the passive female members of the team send to the bullying Mediterranean shipping specialist during his initial attack is: 'You can behave that way if you want to, we won't intervene.' They simultaneously allow themselves to be groomed while also enabling a powerful attack. They also leave their targeted peer without support during the attack and, feeling helpless and powerless in the face of considerable aggression, she protects herself as best she can by removing herself from the situation.

What impact does the European airline specialist's decision to remove herself from the room have on the dynamic evolving between her and the bully? Firstly, it affords her respite from an ongoing abusive outburst. Secondly, it tells the bully that, while she cannot prevent him from speaking, she can take actions to ensure that she doesn't have to listen to what he says. Thirdly, it preserves some of her personal power by sending the message to the bully that she is able to act in her own best interests. Lastly, it tells her peers that she is not prepared to remain in a meeting at which they sit idly by and allow her to be abused. Overall, in a situation in which she is subject to powerful sustained aggression, has no obvious allies, and limited choices for protecting herself, removing herself from the room is a wise thing for the European airlines specialist to do. However, she could remain in the room and make an effective confrontation.

In this case, she would be confronting both the bully and her passive peers. This is a high-risk strategy to employ as it could result in one or more of her peers turning against her due to their discomfort with an on-going and, as they would see it, aggressive argument. However, if she handles it well, the European specialist's confrontation could prove decisive in dissuading the bully from attacking her again in a team meeting. She could wait for the bully to complete his rant and, in a factual and firm tone, say: 'I am quite taken aback by that outburst. It was powerfully aggressive and personally offensive.' She could then move swiftly on to the work agenda to demonstrate to him that his attack did not unsettle her, puncture her self-esteem or remove control from her. This challenge lays down a clear marker to the bully and her passive peers that what he said was unacceptable to her, and that she doesn't want to hear anything like it again.

Key Incident Two: Taking Over the Target's Work

In this incident, the Mediterranean shipping specialist proposes to his peer group that he take over a large part of the European airlines specialist's non-policy work. He makes this proposal at a team meeting with his other peers on a day when his target is on annual leave, fully aware that for a change in work allocation to be enacted every member of the team needs to agree to it. Rather than suggest he re-submit his proposal on a date when the European airlines specialist is present, the other members of the team ratify it then and there. In that moment, they all move from being passive enablers of the bullying to active colluders. Why do they do this?

Each of the non-targeted peers recognises the significant degree of aggression displayed in this meeting by the Mediterranean specialist towards the European airlines specialist. They see it for what it is: a clear power play by a powerfully controlling peer against his target in her absence. Each of them also recognises that they ought to raise objections to his proposal on the grounds that she isn't there. But rather than take this line, each and every one of them colludes with his plan. They actively approve it, apparently without a thought for the impact these actions will have on their absent colleague. Their misguided motivation is their own welfare, and their desire to avoid contesting with their aggressive, bullying peer. They take the view that going along with the wishes of the Mediterranean specialist represents the path of least resistance and, overall, is in their best interests. They fail to recognise that the venality of their actions will work against them in larger and smaller ways.

Firstly, they fail to recognise that they have sent a clear message to the bully that whenever he wants to remove someone's work from that person behind their back, he can do so with the active support of the rest of the peer group. The colluding peers don't stop to think that he could just as easily put a proposal onto the table to remove some of their work from them behind their backs, should he want to. Secondly, they fail to recognise that in actively colluding with him, they are setting up a dynamic in which they hand over power to a ruthlessly aggressive peer, someone who does not recognise or respect the usual boundaries around workplace relationships. Thirdly, they fail to recognise that he is unlikely to be satisfied with the degree of power he has already wrested from them, and is likely to want more.

Far from placating him by giving him what he wants, they have set up a situation where he, and subsequently the bullying African specialist, can dominate their meetings whenever they want to.

What options are open to the European specialist once she learns that her colleagues have agreed to transfer part of her work to the Mediterranean specialist behind her back? Immediately she learns of this ploy, she needs to send an email to the bully, every other peer and the head of underwriting. The email could say: 'I understand that a decision to transfer some of my non-policy work to the Mediterranean shipping specialist was taken while I was on annual leave. The firm's policy states that any decision to re-allocate work from one member of the senior underwriting team to another can only be ratified in the presence of all of the team members. This decision was taken when I was on annual leave, and is invalid. I will therefore retain control of all of my work, including completing the in-house training manual and providing mentoring to all four of my trainees, for the foreseeable future.' She could then print out the email and put it onto the desk of the bully and each of her peers, before making a call to the head of underwriting to draw his attention to the email which will be in his inbox.

Key Incident Three: Attributing False Blame

In this incident, one of the collusive female peers says to the European airlines specialist: 'You make me very uncomfortable in team meetings because you make the Mediterranean specialist angry'. This is a complicated thing to say because it is impossible for the European airlines specialist to 'make' her bullying peer angry. Rather, her bullying peer generates his anger when he wants to, and the actions of the European airlines specialist neither precipitate nor create that anger. These words are an indication of the degree of discomfort which the colluding peer feels about working alongside someone who is routinely abusive and aggressive at work, and with her part in the collusion to remove some of the European specialist's work from her. Rather than confront her own shame at her part in that meeting, rather than learn the skills and find the courage to confront the bullying, rather than place the responsibility for being a bully where it rightly belongs – with the bully – this colluding peer adds insult to injury by blaming the target for the aggression of the bully. She fails to make a distinction between right and wrong, and demonstrates just how fallible she is. How might the European airlines specialist respond?

She could simply state the fact: 'The Mediterranean specialist's temper is his own business. I don't have anything to do with it.' Or she could say: 'I am surprised to hear you say that. The Mediterranean specialist is responsible for his own temper, and no one other than him can influence it.' She could then walk away to denote that the conversation is closed.

Key Incident Four: Abuse in the Corridor

In this incident, the bullying Mediterranean specialist attacks his target a second time. This attack is conducted in public, in full view of colleagues using a busy corridor by a man who is emboldened by the success of his previous attacks. So confident is he of his capacity to behave anyway he likes, whenever he chooses, that he selects a busy corridor as the venue for his next assault, certain that no one present will oppose him. He attacks his target for being incompetent and shoddy in her work, neither of which criticism is justified, both of which are designed to humiliate her in public by a powerfully controlling accuser.

The bully subjects his target to a barrage of unjust censure for the quality of her work, and only ceases his attack when she cleverly suggests that they discuss the issues in private. This is the last thing he wants to do for two reasons. Firstly, by saying they could continue the dialogue in private, she draws his attention to the inappropriateness of his choice of venue for the confrontation. Secondly, none of his criticisms is valid. Rather than have a discussion with her about the ins and outs of his bogus critique, he stomps off in the caricature of an angry man, leaving the target alone in a corridor full of colleagues whom she worries have overheard everything.

Had she wanted to confront him in the corridor, what could the European airlines specialist say? She could wait for the bully to finish speaking and then say: 'I am disappointed to hear you expressing these opinions, but I am not surprised. I'll leave it up to the people in the corridor to form their own conclusions about the quality of your input.' She could then walk away from him.

Key Incident Five: A Second Campaign

In a series of incidents, the African shipping specialist starts to bully the European airlines specialist. He has watched the successful grooming of the team by his male peer, and chooses this moment to strike. Having observed his peer attack the European airlines specialist to her face and behind her back, and no doubt having heard about his attack in the corridor, he decides to commence a campaign against her too. In a series of manoeuvres designed to isolate her and remove influence from her, he introduces new work processes and software when she is absent and doesn't tell her about them. He dismisses her input in team meetings, characterising her words as irrelevant or pointless, and he slanders her behind her back to their joint manager. How does his peer group respond to these bullying tactics?

Predictably, the non-targeted peers acquiesce to the new bully. At different times, they adopt the role of both passive enablers and active colluders. Their passive enabling occurs when they allow his dismissive reactions to the target's sensible and well-considered points to remain unchallenged. Their active collusion occurs when they accept his new software and work processes without recognising the need to involve their absent colleague in these decisions. Since the non-targeted peers had already given so much of their power to the Mediterranean specialist, it is unsurprising that the second bully finds it so easy to commence his own campaign against the unfortunate European airlines specialist.

What can the European airlines specialist do in response to these tactics? When she discovers that new software and work processes have been introduced without her knowledge, she could make it a priority to familiarise herself with them. Then, at the next peer meeting, she could start the proceedings by giving her conclusions about the performance and suitability of the new methods for the team's work. This way of handling things communicates to the African specialist that she hasn't been ruffled by his underhand manoeuvres. It informs him that she will respond to his sneakiness with professionalism, negating his attempt to isolate, control and undermine her.

During meetings, using a tone which conveys a degree of amazement, she needs to challenge every dismissive comment the African specialist makes in response to her suggestions. For instance, when the

African specialist waves his hand to trivialise her recommendation, she could say: 'Can you tell me *exactly in what way* that recommendation doesn't matter?' When he expresses indifference for a risk factor she has highlighted, she could say: 'How could ignoring a clear risk factor be in the best interests of the firm or the customer?'

When she learns that the African specialist has spread misinformation about her to their joint manager, the European specialist needs to act. Either in a telephone call, or face to face, she needs to put the facts on the table for her manager to consider. Speaking in a measured, careful pace, she could say: 'I understand that the African specialist has said that I don't enjoy my job, that have had a public spat with the Mediterranean specialist in a corridor, and that I am a nuisance in team meetings. None of these accounts is accurate. What *is* true is that I still enjoy my job despite some challenges in the team. What is also true is that the Mediterranean specialist stomped up to me in a corridor and made an angry outburst. I was concerned about the incident occurring in public and quickly defused it. The team issues are more complex, and involve the need to have extended debates over relatively straightforward matters in order to arrive at sound underwriting decisions.' Depending on how the head of underwriting responds, the European specialist could then say: 'In my experience, some people lie to themselves, and some people lie to others. I am clear which way round it was in this instance.'

Key Incident Six: Simultaneous Attacks

In this series of incidents, both the Mediterranean and African shipping specialists attack their target in team meetings. Their attacks are separate lines of assault which occur concurrently. The European airlines specialist can be under no illusion about the degree of challenge she faces in team meetings in which two bullies independently attack her at the same time, and all her colleagues turn a blind eye to the assaults.

Team meetings are now completely dominated by two peers whose main aim is to attack their target rather than make sound and prudent decisions about underwriting terms for new policies. This team is in crisis. Its energy goes towards coping with bullying behaviour. Its processes are hampered by the bullying agenda of the two male peers, and its work takes second place to their desire to subjugate their female target. Quite apart from the considerable distress caused to the target, it can only be a matter of time before the senior under-writing team ratifies a policy which exposes the firm to genuine risk, and which backfires on a group of peers who have allowed one member of their team to be relentlessly attacked by two others.

What can the European airlines specialist do about the attacks at the time they occur? Her strongest suit is her ability to convey to the two bullies that their attempts to de-rail her don't work. These two bullies thrive on the bogus sense of 'power' they feel when they think they have punctured her self-confidence or upset her in a meeting. Her willingness to assert her right to be heard, her commitment to calling them to account for their flippant disregard for her input, and her persistence in contesting their bullying behaviour will work greatly in her favour. These actions will cut down the room for manoeuvre open to them, reduce the pleasure they derive from seeing her unset-tled, prove that she is well-equipped with self-confidence, resilience and self-protective skills, and can give as good as she gets.

Inimical Peers: Conclusions

What conclusions can we draw from this case study? Firstly, we can say that the target in this case is unusually ill-fated to work alongside a team of peers who either bully her or enable that bullying. Her dis-tress at being targeted by two separate members of her peer team is compounded by the lethargy of every other member of the team towards her plight. The two campaigns both have the same aim: to undermine her inner-self and negate her influence in the team. In the face of such a challenging situation and, given the limited options available to her for protecting herself, her ability to remain pro-fessional and dedicated to her role are greatly in her favour.

Secondly, we can say that the team of non-targeted peers leave themselves open to a situation in which their team meetings become dominated by the actions of two controlling bullies. Without remov-ing any responsibility for their behaviour from either bully, we can say that the actions of the non-targeted team members make it straight-forward for both bullies to operate unhindered.

Thirdly, we can say that the fundamental mistake of the non-targeted peers was in thinking that by giving the first bully a little of what he wanted – the opportunity to castigate his target in a team meeting – he would be satisfied and desist thereafter. Quite the opposite is true. Rather than be content with that one attack, this bully is encouraged to proceed with his campaign and to escalate it, paving the way for the second bully to commence his campaign. In the end, team meetings become vehicles for aggression and abuse, compromising the well-being of the target, and the quality of decision-making and work produced by the team.

Summary of Key Points from the Chapter

Effective peer relationships are based on mutual respect for one another's work, and goodwill. Under normal conditions, you will work with your peers to keep your relationships viable, deferring to one another based on your differing levels of expertise and skill.

Because you both have equal organisational power, a skilled bullying peer is likely to target you with the intention of undermining your inner self and your reputation. When their attacks are carried out in front of other members of your peer group, each of those peers needs to make decisions about how they will react to the incident at the time. Their choices are to adopt the role of passive enabler, to actively collude with the bullying, or to confront it effectively.

Some of your peers may become passive enablers because they are too afraid to speak up. Others may not know how to confront effectively, remaining silent even though they are horrified by the bullying. Others again misunderstand the situation, believing that they are witnessing something private between you and the bully. Colleagues who passively enable an attack against you may change the way they treat you after the incident. They may do this for complicated reasons which centre on the shame they feel at failing to support you at the time.

A minority of your peers may actively collude with the bully. They may endorse the bullying verbally or non-verbally, or may add bullying comments of their own. Colleagues who actively collude may do this because they dread being targeted and, in a misguided attempt to protect themselves, side with the bully.

Peers who passively enable or actively collude set themselves up for trouble as they send a message to the bully that they will be straightforward people for them to groom and target. Passive enablers and active colluders each give their power to the bully, making themselves vulnerable to attack.

The alternative stance is to confront effectively. An effective confrontation is one which sends the message to the bully that the peer knows how to draw the line, is calling the bully to account, putting the issues back to the bully and providing life-affirming support to you, the target. By verbalising an effective challenge, a courageous peer can also embolden you and other members of the team to find the courage to speak against the bullying as well. The principles highlighted in the chapter for confronting a bullying peer can also be applied to other team bullying dynamics including challenging a bullying manager or a bullying junior team member.

Questions for You to Consider

In this chapter, we have been examining how to respond to a bullying peer. You may now want to apply this material to your own experience by responding to the following questions. You can jot down your answer to each of the following questions in the space below it.

Call to mind an incident in which you were subject to bullying by a peer in your team and the attack was witnessed by at least one other peer.

1. What happened during this incident? What bullying tactics did your bullying peer employ?

2. How did you handle this incident at the time?

3. How did the non-targeted peer(s) who witnessed the assault behave at the time?

4. Which of them adopted the role of passive enabler? Which of them adopted the role of active colluder?

5. Which of them challenged the bullying? How effective were they at confronting the bully? What impact did the confrontation(s) have on you?

6. Looking back on it now, what could you have said or done at the time which would have put the issues back to the more bully more effectively?

7. Looking back on it now, what would you have liked your non-targeted peers to say or do to confront the bully more effectively?

Next Chapter

Chapter 8 explores the issues involved when a campaign is orchestrated by a junior member of the team against those with greater organisational authority than them. It examines the authority issues involved in upward team bullying, highlighting how unresolved issues in the life of the bully contribute to them targeting their manager or supervisor. The chapter highlights a number of ways in which to challenge upwards team bullying, each of which encourages the bully to take responsibility for the unresolved anger in their life and develop a greater level of maturity, so they can work effectively with authority figures.

Chapter 8
When the Bully is More Junior Than You

The Tactics of an Upwards Bully

Upwards bullying occurs when someone more junior than you in the team hierarchy targets you in a campaign. The bully's attack on you, someone with greater organisational authority than them, originates in their *unresolved authority issues and dislike or fear of authority.* The upwards bully is likely to target your leadership, management or supervision. Their tactics can include:

- Challenging your plans, proposals and wishes to question your competence to perform your role.

- Influencing other team colleagues to alter their view of you and take on board a pejorative assessment of your suitability to lead.

- Agreeing to your face that they will undertake certain tasks to an agreed standard, but subsequently failing to do them in an attempt to undermine your plans.

- Attacking you in obviously angry or rage-filled assaults designed to injure your inner self.

- Demonstrating consistent or intermittent disrespect for your style of supervision, management or leadership.

- Blocking progress on tasks for which they are responsible to passively thwart work processes which you oversee.

- Questioning your values or personal conduct to call into question your fitness to carry out your duties.

- Generating plausible sounding 'reasons' why they don't want to follow your lead, each of which represents their wilful refusal to cooperate rather than a genuine objection.

- Misrepresenting innocent incidents involving you, or exaggerating genuine but unimportant errors which you have made, to impugn your character and influence susceptible team members to think less well of you.

A campaign orchestrated by a skilled upwards bully can feel very personal indeed. The upwards bully primarily targets your organisational authority. But, if you are a supervisor, manager or leader who identifies with your role, you can quickly experience self-doubt or become personally destabilised by the attacks. It may help you to know that the upwards bully's actions are derived from their desire to *oppose what authority means to them,* even though the campaign is directed at you as an individual. This distinction may not necessarily lessen the challenge associated with handling a campaign of upwards bullying, but it may give you a different perspective on the motivation of the bully.

Unresolved Authority Issues

Team members who bully upwards are likely to have had past experiences of abusive, dangerous or incompetent leadership. These experiences may have been in their formative years, or could have been from a former time in their working lives. In either case, the upwards bully imports their dislike and fear of these authority figures into the present and plays out those dynamics in their relationship with you.

An upwards bully can operate along a continuum which is characterised by indirect, passive-aggressive behaviour at one end, to rage-filled venomous openly destructive attacks at the other. Being targeted by an upwards bully who is raging and oppositional can be an overwhelming experience, leaving you feeling shocked and paralysed.

Your Authority: The Battleground Between You and an Upwards Bully

The upwards bully makes your right to supervise, manage or lead them the battleground between the two of you. They contest your decisions, refuse to cooperate with your plans, thwart your proposals and oppose you whenever they can. Their aim is to avoid being placed in a situation where, as they see it, they will be vulnerable to either your censure or your disapproval, while also making their defiant dislike of your authority an issue between you. Under the relentless pressure characterised by these dynamics, you may be tempted to concede over some matters simply to keep the peace. But this is not a wise thing to do. It can be exhausting to deal with a persistently rebellious upwards bully who is intent on undermining your reputation, questioning your ability to lead, and contesting the direction you set for the work of the team. But the challenge before you is to find ways of *retaining control of your authority*, especially when you are under pressure.

Your ability to assert your right to supervise, manage or lead *is* the response you need to make at the time of each incident. An incident of upwards bullying does not represent a negotiation with the bully over your right to your authority. Your employer has invested a degree of organisational authority in you, and it is yours to use responsibly for the good of your team and its customers. Hesitating, giving ground to the bully, or accommodating over your right to your authority, will not work well for you. These well-intentioned but flawed strategies, predicated on the idea that you might be able to demonstrate to the upwards bully that you are a reasonable person, will work against you. If you take any of these approaches, the upwards bully is unlikely to come to the conclusion that you are different from their previous abusive authority figures, and desist with their campaign. In fact, they are more likely to continue with it or escalate it because they are encouraged by your lack of resolve. *Asserting your right to your organisational status at the time of an incident is the most effective way to challenge upwards bullying.*

The Impact of Upwards Bullying on Team Dynamics

The aim of an upwards bully is to challenge the authority of you, their supervisor, manager or leader. Their tactics involve attacking you to your face, but they also include talking about you behind your back with other members of the team to alter their opinion of you. A skilled upwards bully will take a snippet of truth about you and dress it up in fabrications, lies and embellishments to suit their purpose. Unsuspecting team colleagues hear the snippet of truth and swallow the rest of the story whole, falsehoods and all. Subsequent team interactions can become challenging for you as you try to get to the bottom of what was said, understand why it was said, handle your own distress at being misrepresented, and persuade your team colleagues about the truth of the matter.

Depending on the persistence and skill with which an upwards bully influences other members of the team against you, the quality of your interactions with specific team members, and the quality of the work produced by your team, can reduce substantially. Specific ways in which team dynamics could alter for the worse include:

- Team members who listen to misinformation about you subsequently expending valuable energy thinking about or discussing your supposed failings with one another, looking for evidence to back up or refute the allegations, and becoming diverted away from concentrating on their work.

- Specific team members becoming less cooperative towards you, failing to work productively with you and refusing to take your lead. Some of the interactions between you and specific team members could become strained and unproductive as these team members demonstrate their growing disrespect for your authority by withdrawing their active support from you.

- The character of team meetings changing, becoming less productive and more troublesome. The tone of these meetings can move away from an active focus on the work issues into sullen disengagement or a refusal to participate on the part of some or all of the members of the team.

- The quality of team outputs becoming compromised as team members allow their growing negative feelings about you to result in poorly executed work. You may need to ask them to re-do certain tasks, or may need to expend an unusual amount of effort trying to get your previously committed team members to engage productively with their work.

All of these distractions undermine the team's work, interfere with the smooth running of team processes, and reduce the team's ability to produce top quality outputs. Dealing with issues like these on a regular basis can become exhausting and distressing for you, as your time becomes thinly stretched. Depending on the circumstances, the greater part of your energy could go towards shoring up your tarnished reputation rather than towards manging your team and its work processes, and the work of the team can be undermined as members of the team start to feel less comfortable working for a supervisor, manager or leader they no longer fully trust, and consequently produce less effective work.

Blocking Progress, Refusing to Cooperate, Undermining Team Effectiveness

Consider the following examples:

- An upwards bully with a considerable degree of rage towards authority figures targets his manager in a campaign of open, forceful bullying. The upwards bully, who is blind to their authority issues, generates numerous criticisms, rebukes and counter-arguments to the perfectly practical plans and proposals of his manager. His objective is to thwart his manager's aims, undermine his authority and reduce his effectiveness. The upwards bully attacks his manager in team meetings, speaks in derogatory terms about him behind his back, and incites other members of the team to bad-mouth him over lunch when their manager is absent. Much of the manager's energy and time is diverted away from his work into lengthy and exhausting arguments with the upwards bully. Each of these discussions is marked by a significant degree of hostility on the part of the bully, and an increasingly weary set of rebuttals by the beleaguered manager. Even when the upwards bully appears to have backed down and agreed to carry out his tasks in accordance with his manager's wishes, he leaves the meeting and does exactly the opposite.

- An upwards bully instigates a stealthy campaign of innuendo and slander against her supervisor. Her main tactic is to incite other members of the team to think less well of the supervisor. These incidents always occur behind the supervisor's back and involve the upwards bully subtly slandering her, portraying her as less competent, less skilled and less able than she is. The bully suggests that the supervisor takes the credit for the team's work, doesn't stand up for them to senior managers, and isn't actively seeking to procure a pay increase for them, something which she has promised to do. Although she has no evidence to back up any of these claims, the upwards bully presents her slanderous allegations as facts and is taken at face value by those of her team colleagues who are willing to believe the worst about their supervisor. The supervisor recognises that the attitude of some of her team members has altered and, misunderstanding the reason for this change of heart, arranges a series of one-to-one meetings with each of them in an attempt to get to the bottom of the issues. She experiences each meeting as a frustrating waste of time, leaving each of them with the distinct impression that she is missing something. Over the next few weeks, the quality of the team's outputs drop and the supervisor is called to her manager's office to explain the dip in performance.

- An upwards bully commences a campaign against her direct manager who is also her employer. The upwards bully simultaneously needs approval from her employer and fears his censure and criticism. Afraid of the latter, but needing the former, the upwards bully is truculent and off-hand to her employer's face, while working against him behind his back. Her covert campaign involves speaking in a derogatory manner about him with anyone in the firm who will listen. During these attempts to 'canvass opinion' the upwards bully calls her employer's judgement into question, challenges the basis of his decision-making, questions his values, and suggests that 'he messes junior employees about.' The management team become aware of these discussions about the supposed failings of the business owner. A lot of management time is spent discussing the ins and outs of the upwards bully's behaviour without anyone in authority actually confronting her. The business owner grows to dislike his meetings with the upwards bully, quickly tiring of her quarrelsome defiance. He decides to stop managing her, and switches her reporting line to another senior figure in the business. Although this manoeuvre means that he himself is no longer the target for the upwards bully's wrath, he has set up his managerial colleague for exactly the same treatment.

In each of these scenarios, the upwards bully is unable to make a distinction between their fear of a previous authority figure and their desire to undermine the authority of their current supervisor, manager or employer. In each case, the upwards bully creates plausible-sounding 'reasons' to question the authority, integrity or conduct of their current authority figure in a series of campaigns which consume the time and energy of the target and, in the third example, also the management team. In the first scenario, the bully orchestrates lengthy arguments with his manager, requiring the authority figure to reiterate his points of view, justify his opinions, and re-argue his case. In the second scenario, the supervisor recognises that something is wrong in her team, and sets up a series of time-consuming and futile meetings in an attempt to remedy the situation. These meeting prove futile, wasting everyone's time, and don't prevent her from being called to her manager's office to explain a drop in her team's performance. In the third scenario, much management time is spent discussing the issues raised by the upwards bully's habit of discussing the supposed faults and failings of the business owner with anyone in the firm who will listen. Eventually, tired of her insolence and petulance, the business owner switches her reporting line to a different senior colleague. This ploy only sets up his colleague for exactly the same degree of challenge.

In all of these scenarios, the targets handle the bullying in a variety of different ways, each of them doing the best they can in a challenging situation. But they all fail to do the one thing which would have enabled them to confront the upwards bully effectively. They all fail to *assert their right to their authority in the moment of an attack.*

On the face of it, *not* asserting authority might seem like a wise strategy. After all, since the battleground chosen by the upwards bully is the authority of the target, surely asserting that authority would make a bad situation worse? This would be the case if the target were to assert their authority in a forceful, aggressive or demeaning way. Any version of these ways of doing things would reinforce all the upwards bully's perceptions about bad or abusive authority and compound the problem. But, if the target uses their authority carefully to draw the line, and require that the bully participate constructively in the meeting while playing back the behaviour which is out of line, the target stands a good chance of handling the incident effectively. Why? Because what the upwards bully *wants* and what they *need* are different.

An upwards bully *wants* to oppose your supervision, management or leadership *because of what you symbolise to them: bad or abusive authority.* But what they *need* is for you to demonstrate to them *that you represent a different kind of authority figure* from their abusive previous experience, one who is fully invested in your authority and able to use that authority with skill, wisdom and generosity, even under pressure. Handling an encounter or, if you need to, repeated encounters with an upwards bully can demonstrate to them that you are not a replica of the abusive authority figure they fear, and that it is time for them to re-direct their energies away from undermining you towards the effective accomplishment of their work.

Let's revisit the three scenarios above to illustrate this principle.

- In the first scenario, a rage-filled upwards bully refuses to cooperate with his manager's proposals, generating numerous criticisms, rebukes and counter-arguments to the perfectly practical plans put on the table by the manager. The manager takes the 'reasons' which the upwards bully generates at face value and debates them. Instead, the manager could play back to his errant team member the aggression, disrespect and refusal to cooperate to which he has been subject and require that he makes a constructive contribution to the meeting. He needs to continue to do this until the upwards bully starts to contribute in a calm and productive manner or, if the upwards bully refuses to do so, tell him to come back when he is ready to contribute straightforwardly. He could say: 'I just heard you respond with contempt and disbelief to a perfectly sound proposal I made. There are no real grounds for such a reaction, and I am putting it straight back to you. What did you mean by it?' Depending on the response he gets, the manager could say: 'I require that, if you are to remain in this meeting, you make a productive contribution to it. If you cannot do that, leave and come back when you are prepared to contribute straightforwardly.'

- In the second scenario, when the supervisor recognises that the atmosphere in her team has altered, she needs to act. She does not know that an upwards bully in the team has been inciting unwise team members to think less well of her behind her back. Nor does she know that this is the context for the reduced performance and altered attitude that she has picked up in team meetings. What the supervisor does know is that something is wrong. Rather than hold an increasingly futile series of one-to-one meetings with each member of the team, the supervisor needs to address the issues *with the entire team present.* She needs to play back to them what she has observed and ask what lies behind the observations she has made. She could sit upright with her head held high and say in a relaxed tone: 'I have noticed that the atmosphere in these team meetings has altered. They are no longer productive and work-focused, and some of you don't contribute very much at all. What is going on?' She then needs to maintain level eye contact with each member of the team, challenging them to speak. Assuming that none of them is likely to do so easily, she needs to press them again. She could say: 'I sense that something is going on which is affecting the work this team is producing. What is it?' She needs to keep them in the room with her until one of them finds the courage to break the silence. Not everyone in the team has sided with the bully and sooner or later someone will speak. How the supervisor handles the ensuing conversation will be a clear test of her authority. But, having brought the issues out into the open at a team meeting, she now stands a good chance of reasserting her authority and demonstrating to the foolish members of her team who colluded with the bully that they have listened to the wrong person. She could say: 'What I am hearing is that some of you doubt that I have been actively pursuing a pay increase for each member of this team. Let me tell you the fact of the matter. On Tuesday, I raised this issue with the MD and I am meeting her again tomorrow to continue the discussions.' Countering each of the slanderous accusations with the facts will enable her to re-assert her right to supervise the team. It will also deal a big blow to the upwards bully's reputation, decisively undermine her credibility with those team colleagues who had supported her, and go a long way to preventing her from continuing with her campaign.

- In the third scenario, the business owner becomes so fed up of the rebellious defiance of the upwards bully that, after discussing the issues at length with his senior colleagues, he moves her reporting line to one of his colleagues. This manoeuvre may well spare him any further assaults, but it sets up his colleague for the same treatment he has received. What else could he have done? When the business owner becomes aware that the upwards bully is 'canvassing opinion' against him, and inciting other people in the firm to collude with him, he needs to confront her. He needs to sit her down and confront her with the facts. Using a measured and calm tone, he could say: 'I understand that you have been working behind my back to suggest to members of the firm that I am an unfit leader. I also have evidence from meetings between the two of us that you regularly contest my views, question my judgement and oppose my plans. You are an employee in my firm. I think its untenable for someone I employ to be using their energy in these ways, and I require you to use your time and your skills only in the service of your job description. If you truly believe I am an unfit person to run and own this business, why are you still working for me?'

In each of these scenarios, the target is not afraid of their authority or otherwise uncomfortable with it. Rather, they take confident actions which enable them to hold onto and use their authority effectively to challenge the campaign against them and lessen its impact on their team. Each of these confrontations is effective because it simultaneously achieves several things. Each confrontation:

- Re-asserts the target's right to supervise, manage or lead.

- Actively demonstrates to the upwards bully that the target is fully invested in their authority and prepared to use it to re-establish control.

- Requires the upwards bully to use their energy, time and skills productively for the good of the team.

- Prevents the upwards bully from continuing to exert influence with members of the wider team.

- Uses the facts to confront slander and lies.

- Avoids the pitfalls of being abusive, angry or belittling towards the bully, actions which would exacerbate the situation.

- Prevents members of the wider team or firm from wasting valuable time and energy discussing slanderous accusations and issues created by the upwards bully's campaign.

- Gives the upwards bully a clear choice: take responsibility for your actions, cease bullying and start to make a valuable contribution to the team or continue to bully and be challenged.

Ambivalence Towards Your Own Authority

In each of the above scenarios, the target is fully invested in their authority, albeit they need to learn to use it wisely to defeat the upwards bully. But what about a situation in which you are not comfortable with your authority and feel ambivalent towards it? Regardless of the degree of force involved in an attack, any ambivalence you may feel towards your own organisational authority can compound the challenge you face in handling upwards bullying. Perhaps you:

- *Don't want to lead, manage or supervise.* You may only be performing the role until someone else is found to take it on long-term. In this case, your ambivalence is about your lack of commitment to your role and consequent organisational authority.

- *Have had your own damaging experiences with immature or incompetent leadership.* You are concerned that, with role models like these, you might also harm a member of your team. In this case, your ambivalence is about your position as an authority figure and the fact that, in your mind, power is primarily an abusive force, not a force for good.

- *Want to maintain a degree of camaraderie and friendship with your team members.* You don't want to adopt the role of a remote, formal authority figure. You try to maintain a balance between preserving rapport with your team members and leading them. In this case, your ambivalence is about a conflict between wanting warm bonds with your team members and the need to maintain a professional distance in order to manage them effectively.

In all of these scenarios, responsibility for targeting you remains firmly with the upwards bully. But in each of them, your challenge at handling the upwards bullying is complicated by the fact that *you are uncomfortable with your own authority*. Your discomfort may mean that you don't hear a bullying attack as a direct assault on your right to lead. Or, if you do hear it that way, you may be unwilling to assert your right to that authority because you are conflicted about it. The upwards bully may find it more straightforward to target you successfully because you hesitate, display uncertainty or avoid the confrontation they need to have. Let's see how these themes play out in a longer and more complicated example.

Case Study 8: Upwards Bullying

A busy independent boutique employs a team of six employees. Three of its employees have worked at the boutique for a year and three others are long-standing members of staff. They work well together, displaying high degrees of cooperation and team work. One of the long-standing employees manages the shop floor on behalf of the owner of the boutique. It is her job to manage the team, make sure that customers are handled promptly and courteously, and that the shop floor runs efficiently and effectively. The boutique owner rarely comes onto the shop floor, preferring to run the business from the anonymity of his office at the back of the shop.

The three newer members of staff get on well with one another. They go shopping in their lunch breaks and chat to one another about the ins and outs of serving customers and their experiences of their day. As they live in the same part of town, two of them regularly take the bus home together after work. The manager observes the camaraderie of the three juniors and feels slightly jealous that she has not managed to strike up a similar degree of rapport with either of the two long-standing members of staff, albeit they all get on well together as a team. Her management style is characterised by a degree of method and order, a preference for planning, and a desire to keep her records and paperwork up-to-date and accurate. Under normal circumstances, she has no trouble getting them to buy-in to her ideas and plans, and securing high degrees of active cooperation from her team members.

A week into the busy summer period, one of the three juniors starts to bully the boutique manager. The initial grooming attack takes the form of the bullying junior pointing out a series of 'errors' that she claims the manager has made on the inventory of new stock, criticisms which she makes using a tone of voice which is cutting and calculated to undermine her manager's confidence. The manager is able at her job but lacks obvious assertion. She prefers to work with colleagues who are good natured, easy to collaborate with and who do things on the basis of goodwill. When she is attacked by her junior team member, she initially feels confused but doesn't bridle or react with any outward show of anger. In the seconds after being bullied, she wonders whether she has genuinely made an error and, instead of reprimanding her colleague for speaking to her in a cutting tone, she busies herself re-checking the inventory and doesn't confront her at all.

The manager mentions the incidents to one of the other long-standing employees who shrugs and says: 'Don't worry about it'. She mentions the same incident to the other long-standing employee and is disappointed again when this colleague tells her that 'she is being overly sensitive'. Over the next week, as the campaign progresses, the bullying member of staff extends her tactics to include attacking her over lunchtime sandwiches for 'having her head in the clouds' and 'only coming to work to have people to chat to'. The manager does not know how to respond to these snide remarks, and feels both dismayed and distressed that no one speaks up for her when she is attacked in their hearing. She is hard-working and conscientious and feels unfairly singled out for criticisms which she thinks are without foundation. But she lacks the confidence to say or do anything about it. She continues to mention the attacks to her long-standing colleagues whenever she can, but none of them is prepared to talk with her about the situation and, on each occasion, the manager feels dejected for bringing up a subject no one else engages with. As the campaign progresses, no one in the team seems to notice how demoralised and tired she looks. Whenever she tries to bring the subject up with one of her colleagues, the response is a confusing combination of 'what are you making such a fuss about?' and disinterest. Worse still, she finds that the other two juniors become surly with her and are slow to react to her instructions.

The manager decides that she must appeal to the boutique owner so she goes to his office at the back of the shop to tell him what is happening. It takes a lot of courage for her to do this but she is confident that, if she puts her points across professionally and straightforwardly, she will be heard. The boutique owner does not interrupt her while she relates the facts to him and lets her complete her narrative. Then he gets up, opens his office door and calls across the shop floor to the bullying junior who is attending to paperwork by the till. The boutique owner invites her to come into his office. The manager is horrified when she hears her employer say these words, and stutters that she'd rather that didn't happen. She starts to back away towards the open door just as the bullying junior enters the room. The boutique owner shuts the door, tells the bullying junior that the manager has made some complaints about her, and says that he wants to hear her side of the story. During the next twenty seconds, the bullying junior launches into a controlled but vicious attack on the manager in which she calls her 'work-shy', 'careless' and 'barely present to her duties'. The manager is so stunned at this turn of events that she can't find anything to say. Overwhelmed that her attempt to protect herself has been hijacked by her assailant in front of her boss, she struggles for breath and goes cold. The bullying junior completes her criticism of the manager's conduct and performance before turning to the boutique owner. She tells him that she has work to do. Then she walks out of the boutique owner's office leaving the door open while the manager spirals into a vortex of anxiety and self-doubt.

Upwards Bullying: Analysing the Team Dynamics

Let's analyse the dynamics which play out between the bullying junior member of the boutique staff and the manager, and between the two of them and the boutique owner. In this example, the three junior members of the team get on well together, enjoying friendly and close working connections. When one of them starts to bully the manager of the boutique, the unfortunate manager finds it hard to stand up to her assailant, and discovers that neither of her two long-standing colleagues cares about her misfortune. Their reactions include telling her she is being too sensitive, and that she shouldn't worry about being spoken to harshly by a junior member of the team. As the campaign against her escalates, she finds it more and more difficult to assert herself, and loses more and more authority around the shop. Conflict-averse and unsupported, she decides to approach the business owner for assistance. Her well-intentioned but naïve attempt to gain help backfires badly as the business owner invites the upwards bully into his office to hear her side of the story. The bullying junior member of the team takes full advantage of this opportunity, and in a wide-ranging, vicious attack portrays the manager as lazy and incompetent. The manager is blind-sided by this turn of events. As the bullying junior declares that she has work to do and turns to leave the business owner's office, the manager spirals into anxiety and self-doubt, her reputation in tatters.

The Challenges Faced by the Manager

The manager is able at her job but ambivalent about her authority. Her management style is methodical, systematic and conscientious. She manages the shop efficiently and builds effective working relationships with her colleagues, all of whom appear to work hard and get on with their jobs. But she has one glaring vulnerability which works against her when she becomes subject to upwards bullying. *She has an ambivalent relationship with her own authority.* She prefers to work with team members who implicitly recognise her role as their manager, are willing to take the lead from her and consequently choose to defer to her wishes. This way of handling things means that she rarely needs to reprimand anyone, can ask different members of staff to carry out certain tasks as and when they need doing, and feels sure that they won't need to be asked twice. She doesn't like conflict and has woefully under-developed conflict-handling skills. Her deficits in this area are considerable, but in the period before the bullying commences, in a harmonious and rapport-oriented team, she manages the team and the shop floor without difficulty and experiences a high degree of cooperation from her team members.

The manager's discomfort with authority extends to both her authority as a leader and her authority as a person. This combination of vulnerabilities leaves her unable to defend herself professionally or personally when she becomes subject to upwards bullying. In the moments after being groomed, she feels confused and wonders if the accusation that she has made a series of errors on the inventory, for all that it was put in unduly harsh tones, may contain some truth. Instead of calling her junior colleague to account for being hostile and insubordinate, she busies herself with the inventory to see if she has made any errors. The thought that she might have done weighs heavily on her mind. Her management style depends to some degree on her being on top of the paperwork so that she can manage risk and ensure quality.

The manager neither reprimands her bullying junior at the time of her grooming attack, nor subsequently speaks to her about the outcome of her investigation into the inventory. Instead, she turns a blind eye to her own abuse, allowing the incident of grooming to go unchallenged. Had she found a way to confront her junior team member at the time of the grooming or shortly afterwards, she may have gone some way towards preventing an escalating campaign against her. As it is, she is unable to confront her assailant who, recognising the vulnerability of her target, moves swiftly into a campaign. As the campaign progresses and the manager fails to repel any of the attacks against her, she turns to both of the long-standing employees and, eventually, her employer for support. Her desire to gain the support of her shop floor colleagues is understandable. She is disappointed when neither of them is prepared to acknowledge the campaign against her, or discuss the issues it raises. But her decision to approach her employer, a man who routinely avoids contact with the people he employs, is more problematic. What could account for this decision?

Part of the answer is her growing desperation at being bullied. Recognising her need for support, and accepting that neither of her long-standing colleagues is prepared to help her, she turns to the only other senior person in the shop. Her decision to do this is predicated on a number of assumptions, and is a clear indicator of her confusion about her own authority and the nature of authority in general. She assumes that her boss, a man with greater organisational status than her, *must* know what to do to help her. She reasons that he is senior to her, he is more experienced in business than her, and he employs the bullying junior member of the team. She assumes, therefore, that he must be someone who has influence over the upwards bully and that, provided she puts her case well, he will intervene on her behalf. She approaches her employer from the point of view of a child approaching a parent. She fails to factor in his woeful lack of skill with people, his disinterest in the day-to-day work of the shop, and his strong preference for confining himself to his office, alone. She sets herself up for a renewed assault which damages her credibility and self-esteem, this time in front of him. Had she not been subject to a skilled campaign of upwards bullying, none of these vulnerabilities would matter. But she is subject to assault by a powerful, skilled foe and these specific vulnerabilities work very much against her.

Lastly, the manager is also faced with the knowledge that the two non-bullying juniors in the team, both of whom are friends with the upwards bully, alter their behaviour towards her. They are no longer straightforward to deal with and don't easily take direction from her. Their own latent antipathy towards 'bad authority' is engaged by the slanderous tactics of their bullying friend, and both of them display a degree of sullenness towards the boutique manager. Without ever refusing to perform tasks she allocates to them, they are nonetheless slow to react to her instructions. As well as dealing with the fact that she is being bullied, the boutique manager also faces the fact that the rapport-oriented and harmonious nature of the team, something which she cherished, has disappeared.

The Mind-Set of the Bullying Junior Team Member

The bullying junior member of the team has worked at the boutique for some time. She has built enjoyable and effective relationships with her two junior colleagues, spending lunchtimes with them and travelling back home on the bus with one of them. Her period of employment has given her plenty of time to observe her manager at work. She notices the way in which her manager glances jealously in the direction of the three junior friends in the team. She observes the way that she prefers to do things: through rapport, active cooperation and goodwill. She recognises that her manager doesn't like conflict and doesn't confront. In the friendly and helpful atmosphere of the team, she may not need to confront or handle conflict very often. But the observations of the would-be bully go beyond the simple iden-tification of issues in her manager's working life. They go towards preparation for a campaign of upwards bullying.

The junior member of the team bides her time, and then strikes. She selects the busy summer period as the timing for her initial act of grooming, aware that her manager is hard pressed with the extra work vacationing customers bring to the boutique. She selects the inventory as the vehicle through which to attack her manager. This is a calculated manoeuvre by a cunning foe. Should she succeed in unsettling her manager over her record-keeping, the would-be upwards bully knows that she would likely strike a blow at her self-confidence and composure. Her judgement is spot on. Her manager's energy does go towards making sure that she hasn't made an error, and *she fails to confront the equally important issue of the hostility of her junior team member.* The would-be bully is pleased to observe this reaction, and immediately moves from grooming into a campaign.

What motivates her to attack the manager? The bullying junior member of the team is motivated by a combination of her powerful antipathy for authority and her contempt for, as she sees it, a weak manager. Her unresolved, latent aggression towards authority figures crystallises into a powerful urge to bully. She opposes her manager on principle, for primarily emotionally derived reasons, making her manager's personal and professional authority the battleground between them. She attacks her manager's work, conduct and management of the boutique, initially targeting her record-keeping and paperwork, before moving on to target the quality of her interactions with the other members of the team. The motivation behind her attacks is her *strong despising of what she regards as weak leadership,* something which is difficult for the manager to combat as her style is naturally understated and low-key. However, even an understated and low-key manager can learn to use their authority to *assert their right to lead*, and this is something which the manager does not do. Instead, she appeals first to her long-standing colleagues, and subsequently to her employer, and finds that she loses power on each occasion.

Each time she does this, as opposed to handling the bullying at the time it occurs, the manager gives greater power to the bullying junior member of the team. The bullying junior observes her manager's inability to respond to her attacks with any degree of authority, and is encouraged to attack again. Equally, given the ease with which she extends her campaign to include an attack on the manager in the business owner's office, the junior bully learns that she can manipulate her employer's perceptions as well. She carefully stores that piece of knowledge away for use on a subsequent occasion.

Lastly, the bullying team member is well aware of the impact she would have on her target should she successfully incite her two junior colleagues to think less well of their manager. She takes advantage of their lunchtimes together, and her journeys home on the bus with one of them, repeatedly to drop the thought into their minds that their manager is not a good person to work for. Her foolish colleagues buy-in to her slanderous campaign and, through their altered behaviour towards their manager, demonstrate to her that they don't respect her as much as they used to do.

The Passivity of the Long-Standing Members of Staff

The other two long-standing members of staff are largely uninterested in the campaign against the manager. As the campaign against her proceeds, the manager approaches each of them, looking for a sounding board and validation that what is happening to her is untoward and worthy of concern. But both of the non-targeted long-standing employees reacts with either a suggestion that their manager is over-reacting, or a banal comment to the effect that she shouldn't worry about it. This combination of disinterest, disengagement and apathy leaves the beleaguered manager without any obvious form of support among her more senior colleagues. Neither of them is willing to engage with what is happening to her because they too are scared that they might also be targeted by the bullying junior employee, someone whose bullying methods they have observed with quiet alarm. While their concern is well founded and understandable, *their conclusion that they become safer by ignoring the fact that they have a bully in the team is quite incorrect*. It may *easier* to avoid confronting this fact, but it is *not safer*. The bully could target either of them too, whether or not they actively support the target of her current campaign. Since neither of the long-standing team members is willing to discuss or even acknowledge the reality of the campaign against her, the manager is effectively stymied.

The Irresponsibility of the Boutique Owner

In desperation, the manager takes the bold but deeply flawed, foolhardy step of turning to the boutique owner hoping for a fair hearing. She has no knowledge about the way in which her withdrawn and semi-reclusive employer might handle her disclosure that she is being targeted by a junior member of the team. But she is not expecting the devastating turn of events which the boutique owner allows to unfold in his office, in which she is assaulted again this time in front of her boss. What could account for the boutique owner's behaviour?

The boutique owner has worked with the manager for a long time. He relies on her to run the shop floor for him, a set of tasks he dislikes and wants to avoid. He prefers to keep himself to himself in his office, handling the orders, accounts and marketing. He does not like dealing with employees or customers. Indeed, he does not like dealing with people at all. Comfortable with the low-key task-oriented style of the manager, and the quiet efficiency with which she manages the shop floor, he leaves all that side of the business to her. When she tells him about the incidents which have upset her so much, he immediately feels out of his depth. Insensitive and poor with people, he does not understand why his manager should be upset, and can't be bothered to enquire further. In his mind, he has three options:

- *Take what his manager says seriously:* which would imply that he must speak with the bullying junior member of his team, take action against her if she has been mistreating the manager, and deal with the fall-out which this uncomfortable set of circumstances would create among the members of his team. This is a deeply unappealing option for the boutique owner to take as it would involve him in dealing with a series of, as he sees it, disputes between people.

- *Play down what the manager is telling him:* which would imply that he must either call her to account for exaggerating a story about the junior employee, or take the line that this is a private matter between the two of them. This is a more palatable option for him to take, as it would involve him pushing the issues under the carpet so he can ignore them.

- *Turn the situation to his advantage:* which would imply that he doesn't care whether the manager is telling the truth or not, provided he can bring this issue to a speedy end once and for all, thereby avoiding the need to take decisive action or get involved. This is a much more palatable option for him, as it would mean that he could get back to his paperwork.

In the split-second available to him to make up his mind, the boutique owner decides on the third option. He does not want to get involved in a messy situation between two members of his team. He can't be bothered with the hassle of determining whether the manager is being bullied or whether the two of them simply don't like one another. In his mind, he characterises the issues between them as a personal spat which has been inappropriately brought to him. He simultaneously fails to investigate the issues and leaps to a precipitous and wrong-headed conclusion. Rather than delve into it all, he abrogates responsibility for discerning the truth, decides to invite the junior member of the team into his office so she can have her say, and abandons the manager to a further assault. He paves the way for the campaign against the manager to continue for as long as the bullying junior wants to orchestrate it and, should she want to, for the bullying junior to continue to manipulate his perceptions subsequently on any number of issues. Indeed, she may even target him in a campaign of upwards bullying. The boutique owner demonstrates a total lack of sensitivity towards the dynamics at play on the shop floor, and a degree of irresponsibility towards his own business which is unusual.

Effective Confrontations for the Manager to Make at the Time of Each Attack

When she is groomed, it is vital that the manager challenge the substance of the accusation that she has made errors on the inventory, and the fact that she is being spoken to by her junior team member in a derogatory and openly hostile manner. These two confrontations will preserve her *personal authority* and her *status as the manager of the boutique.* With some feeling, she could say: 'I don't expect to be spoken to like that by a member of my staff. *If* an error has been made on the inventory, I will let you know.' This confrontation achieves two things for her. Firstly, it makes it crystal clear that she is not to be addressed in such an openly hostile manner again. Secondly, it retains her control of the issues surrounding the inventory. It is now up to her to go back to her junior team member after checking the inventory, or not. If she wants to, again with some feeling, she could say: 'I have checked the inventory. There are no errors in it. If you have any *evidence* that there are issues with it in future, you may tell me but you will need to remember that you are at work and I am the manager of this boutique.' This confrontation makes a clear distinction between the slanderous accusation delivered by the bullying junior and actual evidence of an error. It also reinforces the fact that the manager is the manager, and expects to be addressed in a respectful way. This effective response to the would-be bully's act of grooming may well have been sufficient to dissuade her from proceeding to a campaign.

Upwards bullying: conclusions

Once the campaign has commenced, it is vital that the manager challenge the upwards bully at the time of every attack. Should her assailant attack her over lunch for 'having her head in the clouds' and 'only coming to work to have people to chat to' the manager needs to confront straightaway. These attacks are conducted in front of other members of staff, and the manager risks losing authority and credibility with them should she avoid the confrontation. She could put her sandwiches down onto the table with slow deliberation, before turning to the bullying junior. In carefully modulated tones, to denote that she feels anger but is choosing not to get angry, she could say: 'I come to work to earn my salary and give value to my employer. Those are the only reasons for coming to work that are valid in my book, and they are what I expect from the members of this team. Why are *you* here?' This confrontation is effective because it avoids the pitfall of directly addressing the bullying remarks made by the upwards bully, while comprehensively refuting them. It also enables the manager to turn the conversation back onto the upwards bully, challenging her to explain herself.

The boutique manager also needs to tackle the altered attitude towards her among her other two junior team members. Recognising that they have been listening to gossip and slander, and that it has caused each of them to disrespect her, the boutique manager needs to speak to them separately. In each confrontation, using a firm and factual tone, she could say: 'I have observed you becoming slow to react to instructions I give you, and being surly around me. Since you didn't used to behave like this, I have formed the view that you have allowed your opinion of me to be influenced. What exactly is it that you hold against me?' This confrontation makes it clear that while the junior may have been unduly influenced, she is still responsible for her opinion. It requires her to come clean and, in an adult manner, talk about the issues with her manager. It also successfully re-asserts her manager's authority over her. It is highly unlikely that either junior will want to speak openly about their altered attitude, and more likely that they want to get the interview over with as soon as possible so they can return to their work. But it is equally true that they are unlikely to be surly or off-hand with their manager again, and will be more circumspect in deciding what input from their bullying colleague to believe and what to ignore.

Should the upwards bully attack her in front of her employer, the manager is in a prime position to turn the bullying remarks to her advantage. The bullying junior says that her manager is 'workshy', 'careless' and 'barely present to her duties'. The manager could turn to her employer and say: 'That is a clear example of what I have been talking about. You and I both know that I run the shop floor efficiently and effectively.' She could then stand there with an incredulous expression on her face, requiring her employer to take the issues seriously.

Summary of Key Points from the Chapter

Team members who bully upwards do so out of a combination of their fear or dislike of previous authority figures, and their unresolved feelings about these issues. They import these dynamics into their current relationship with you, targeting you because of what your leadership symbolises to them. Any ambivalence you may feel towards your own authority will compound the challenges you face in combatting the attacks.

Upward bullying attacks can be conducted on a continuum which extends from rage-filled, venomous and openly hostile at one end to slanderous, covert and subtle at the other end. The aim of the upwards bully is to cast doubt over your ability to lead, to question your judgement and to undermine your authority. They may do this by questioning your values, casting aspersions on your character, or refusing to cooperate with your plans and proposals. Upwards bullies can be adept at generating 'reasons' why your suggested way of handling tasks won't work. But none of these 'reasons' are genuine. Instead, they are the bully's way of thwarting your plans, contesting your wishes and seeking to prevent you from having the influence you need with the rest of the team.

Many upwards bullies are successful in influencing non-bullying team colleagues to think less well of you, or to actively disrespect you, outcomes which can seriously compromise the quality of the team's work, and make your interactions with some team members fraught and straining.

It is vital that you confront the bully and prevent the team's valuable time and energy being wasted on discussions about your supposed failings and deficiencies. The optimal way of confronting an upward bully is by *asserting your right to lead in the moment of an attack.* Your aim in confronting the upwards bully is to actively demonstrate to the bully that you are fully invested in your authority, unafraid to draw the line, and require them to participate in team activities in a productive and useful way.

Upwards bullies who alter the views other members of the team hold about you are likely to conduct this part of their campaign behind your back. In this case, once you sense that there is an issue in the team which you need to get to the bottom of, present your observations about the altered atmosphere to the entire team. Require them to put the issues on the table and be prepared to wait until someone speaks. Then use the facts to refute slander and falsehood, unmasking the upwards bully in front of those members of the team who allied with them.

The most counter-productive response you could give would be to belittle, demean or become abusively angry with the upwards bully. These reactions will reinforce their view that authority is always bad and may result in an escalation of their campaign against you.

Questions for You to Consider

In this chapter, we have been examining how to respond to an upwards bully. You may now want to apply this material to your own experience by responding to the following questions. You can jot down your answer to each of the following questions in the space below it.

Call to mind an incident in which you were subject to bullying by a junior member of your team.

1. What happened during the incident? What bullying tactics did the upwards bully employ?

2. How did you handle this incident at the time?

3. Which other of your team members were present at the time of the attack? How did they react to it?

4. To what extent did you lose authority with members of the team as a result of this attack?

5. Looking back on it now, what could you have said at the time of the attack which would have created a more effective and decisive confrontation?

6. To what extent do you feel comfortable with your authority? To what extent did your ambivalence contribute to the dynamics you have just been considering?

Next Chapter

Chapter 9 explores how to bully-proof yourself by rebuilding your self-confidence and self-belief even if a campaign against you is on-going. It explores practical ways to develop your resilience skills, exploring the role that making a formal complaint might make in your recovery from team bullying. The chapter explores the pitfalls of waiting for someone to rescue you, and demonstrates that true rescue involves you recognising the ways in which you give your power away to the bully and building life-enhancing dynamics into your life instead.

Chapter 9
Becoming Bully-Proof: Rebuilding Your Self-Belief and Self-Confidence

The Dual Challenges of Team Bullying

Being subject to team bullying involves you with a dual challenge, and demands that you handle both challenges simultaneously. Your first difficulty originates in the world outside yourself. It can comprise:

- Assaults against your inner self orchestrated by the bully.

- Damage to your reputation engineered by the bully.

- Deteriorating relationships with your team colleagues which can leave you feeling isolated and alone.

Your second difficulty originates in the world inside yourself. It can comprise your:

- Tumbling self-confidence and self-esteem.

- Increasingly self-critical beliefs, thoughts and feelings.

- Diminishing faith in yourself and escalating negativity towards yourself, which can result in high levels of anxiety and self-doubt.

Those of you with experience of severe trauma from team bullying will recognise the difficulty of trying to summon sufficient energy, enthusiasm and willpower to get through a demanding day at work. You may feel that you have no respite from the effort you have to make each day, and the pressure you are subject to. Rather than being characterised by rest and relaxation, your time off can feel insufficient. You may be unable to rest, regroup and relax and, before you know it, you are bracing yourself for the strain of the next working day. The relentless need to cope day after day can be exhausting.

And yet recovery *is* possible. It is possible – and I say this with immense empathy and compassion – to rebuild your self-belief and self-confidence even while a campaign is on-going. It is possible to make the courageous decision to lay claim to your own personal power, and seize the right to express that power to its fullest extent. It is possible to reject any negative, unkind and unjust self-judgements in favour of realistic, fair and compassionate ones, and enjoy the considerable life-enhancement that follows. It is possible to defeat the bullying, confound the active colluders, and refuse to be cowed by the passive enablers in your team. It is possible to feel good about yourself, despite being subject to team bullying. And it is possible for *you* to succeed in doing all these things, even if you don't believe it right now.

Recovery from Team Bullying

Recovery from team bullying involves:

- Healing your emotional self.

- Challenging your mental self.

- Learning new self-protective behavioural skills.

This book has focused extensively on the last of these components. Let's now consider the first two components of your healing journey.

Processing Trauma

Trauma is the result of overwhelming emotional experiences from which you cannot easily move on. These emotional reactions are too intense to be processed using the coping strategies you normally employ in your day-to-day life, and they remain undigested, raw and unprocessed in your system. As we saw in Chapter 3, unprocessed trauma can create a series of debilitating and energy-sapping symptoms.

Healing from overwhelming emotional experience involves processing the residual emotion, identifying what the traumatising experiences meant to you, and then leaving those experiences where they belong: in the past. As you process traumatic emotion so your debilitating symptoms abate, until eventually they are no longer a feature of your life.

Some of you may be able to find strategies which enable you to process trauma by yourself, facilitated by activities such as spending time on a retreat or having a short break in an area of outstanding natural beauty or playing vigorous sports. There are many ways to do it, and you will find a method which works for you. Others of you may be able to process trauma in dialogue with an intimate friend or family member. In this case, the safety of the relationship enables you to talk through what happened with an empathic confidante and find closure from the distress. However, those of you with experience of severe trauma may need to find a practitioner with trauma-relief qualifications to assist you with this part of your recovery. In this case, their specialist knowledge and trauma-relief techniques can enable you to process deeply held emotion safely and effectively.

Healing from trauma provides you with the tools to create a mental self which is realistic, fair and compassionate – a combination which is powerfully self-protective against team bullying.

The Power of Your Mind

The main battleground between you and the bully is *what goes on in your mind.* What you believe about yourself and your work *is* your shield against the lies and slander that the team bully generates during their campaign. It is vital that you recognise this fact because your greatest source of power against bullying lies inside your own head.

What you believe can either fuel your emotional distress both at the time of an attack and subsequently, or it can negate the impact of that bullying attack entirely. A bully who tells you that 'your work is rubbish', that you are 'a useless member of the team', and that the organisation would be 'better off employing someone else' is quite deliberately targeting your inner self: your self-esteem and your self-confidence. Their bullying strategy is to impact what you *feel* about yourself because, if they can do that, they have a good chance of impacting what you *believe* about yourself. So, if you refuse to let the bully impact your inner world, if you decide instead that the final say about your work quality and your value as a person rests with you and you alone, you will go a long way towards disarming the bully and rendering their attack impotent. Bullies who recognise that their target:

- Knows their own mind

- Isn't punctured by their bullying assaults

- Doesn't easily relinquish their personal power

usually recognise that they have met their match and desist. The healing power of even a single, effective confrontation to bullying remarks, delivered with powerful body language, can work wonders for you.

Confidence is a Learned Skill

Self-belief, self-confidence and resilience are all sets of learned skills. No one is born with high levels of any of these attributes. Rather, people who display 'natural' self-confidence, self-belief and resilience have learned what they need to do to maintain high levels of these traits. Equally, when their confidence takes a knock, they know what to do to reinstate their levels of self-belief, self-confidence and resilience back towards their optimum levels. In my work, I focus on facilitating clients to rebuild their self-confidence and self-belief, and assist them to develop their resilience skills. No matter how successful they were prior to being bullied, these clients leave coaching with greater levels of self-belief, self-confidence and resilience than they enjoyed before they were bullied because they have worked to create buoyant levels of all three qualities.

The benefits of acquiring these wonderful bully-proofing skills can be life-changing, especially for those of you who are vulnerable to being groomed and bullied. Learning to own your personal power to its fullest extent results in you behaving assertively and confidently quite naturally every day. These attributes can dissuade would-be bullies from grooming you, and enable you to rebuff with conviction any attempts to bully you. These skills are all learned and learnable, and they can be yours with a little dedication and persistence.

This chapter will show you how to replace self-defeating beliefs with powerful life-enhancing alternatives that enable you to withstand and defeat team bullying. It will demonstrate that, no matter how challenging your situation is, you can turn it around given time, a clear commitment on your part to rebuilding your self-confidence, and a desire on your part to develop your resilience skills. You don't necessarily have to work with a practitioner to achieve these aims, although those of you who have been severely impacted by team bullying may opt to do so.

But before we examine how to acquire these bully-proofing skills, let's take a sideways step to explore one pitfall that you would do well to avoid. That is the pitfall of waiting or expecting to be rescued.

The Pitfall of Waiting or Expecting to be Rescued

Waiting or expecting to be rescued occurs when you feel so beleaguered and powerless that you want someone to appear and save you from the situation of being targeted by a team bully. You might want someone with more organisational authority than the bully to rescue you, perhaps the bully's boss or a senior manager in your organisation. You might want the rescuer to be a practitioner from HR who will investigate your formal complaint, validate your position and require the bully to change their ways. Or you may have no clear idea of who the rescuer might be, but still want them to appear, support you, confront the bully and make the issues go away.

These are understandable thoughts to have. They stem from a concern on your part that you, the target, don't have the personal power required to compel the bully to stop bullying, and from an expectation that the rescuer does. However understandable it can be to generate thoughts about being rescued, they are futile thoughts to entertain. They can cause you to waste precious energy feeling angry that your rescuer hasn't appeared, and feeling resentful towards colleagues or managers for failing to take control of the situation on your behalf. The belief that you are helpless can be deeply buried, but recognising its presence and challenging it will enable you to divert your energy and internal resources into more effective, problem-solving directions – ones which will enable you to rescue yourself.

True rescue occurs when you:

- Recognise the ways in which you currently give your power away to the bully.

- Replace ineffective behaviours with new skills which allow you to retain control of your power and protect yourself at the time of an attack.

- Create lasting life-enhancing dynamics by exchanging false, harsh, self-critical beliefs with more realistic, fair and compassionate ones, ones which will inevitably protect you and promote your well-being.

Seen from this angle, you have everything to gain and nothing to lose by rescuing yourself.

Your Recovery Goal

Your recovery goal is to lay claim to your personal power and learn to express that power to its fullest extent every day so that you use confident, assertive behaviour as a matter of course. Even those of you who have a hard time using assertive behaviour and who dislike conflict can learn to do this, given effective input, commitment and persistence.

In the context of repeated attacks on you by a team bully, expressing your personal power to its fullest extent means:

- Taking responsibility for what you believe to be true about yourself, so that you can refute untrue bullying remarks and refuse to let the bully undermine your inner self.

- Recognising that you generate your feelings about yourself from within, and that you have a choice about what you feel about yourself regardless of what the bully says to you or about you.

- Recognising that any negative and life-defeating beliefs you hold about yourself can fuel your emotional distress at being bullied.

- Deciding to replace negative or life-defeating beliefs with life-enhancing alternative beliefs.

- Deciding you can refute any lies, slanders, falsehoods or half-truths which the bully generates about you so that you can confront mis-information without feeling overwhelmed and distressed.

- Choosing to retain your composure at the time of an attack and saying something that demonstrates that you are not thrown, flustered or upset by the bullying remarks directed at you.

- Repeatedly demonstrating to the bully that you will not be cowed, intimidated or fooled into believing the nonsense they generate, and that you retain full authority over your life and well-being.

- Laying claim to your right to be treated with respect at work under any and all circumstances and, when this is not forthcoming, con-fronting the disrespectful or abusive behaviour.

Learning to live your life in conjunction with these principles makes it more likely that you will find an effective rejoinder to a bullying remark in the moment of an attack. Your effective rejoinder will impact the bully, alter the bullying dynamic in your favour and could dissuade that bully from ever targeting you again in the future. But, an effective rejoinder will also have an immediate and lasting beneficial impact on your well-being too. It will give a boost to your self-confidence, raise your self-esteem and contribute valuably to your healing.

So, how do you learn to live in conjunction with the principles set out above?

Replacing Self-Defeating Beliefs with Life-Enhancing Beliefs

The first step is to recognise that little or nothing which the bully says to you as part of their campaign is likely to be true. Some bullying attacks may contain an element of truth dressed up in distortions and fabrications. But, in the main, bullying remarks do not consist of facts or the truth about you. Seen from this angle, the words a bully uses during an attack cease to hold as much threat as they do when you feel compelled to take them seriously. Your change of attitude towards those remarks gives you strength, and enables you to use your energy to formulate an effective confrontation.

Currently, some of you may struggle to believe this. You may find it a challenge to generate any thoughts about yourself which are *not* negative. You may dwell on your weaknesses and areas of vulnerability and, worse still, the bully may have an instinct for those areas of your performance too, exploiting your self-doubt whenever they can. But the fact remains that no matter what skills or attributes you may need to develop, you do not deserve mistreatment. You do not deserve to be spoken to by a colleague with disrespect or to be subject to abuse. From this standpoint, bullying remarks can never really be about you even if you do genuinely have aspects of your work performance that would benefit from further development. Bullying remarks are always about the mindset of the bully, reflecting their desire to denigrate and demean.

The second step is to acknowledge that skilled bullies can be extremely quick to pick up on your areas of self-doubt, negative self-belief and fear in your life, and on genuine areas for development in your performance. A bully who has intuited the presence of any pre-existing issue in your life may feel highly motivated to target you in that area of vulnerability. Their bullying remarks carry all the more threat because they are deliberately aimed at an area in which you feel under-skilled, on the back foot or deficient. *Because you already believe it, or fear it might be true, the bully's attack has an impact on you*. By contrast, if you were able to dismiss the attack immediately as patently false, it wouldn't pierce you, although you would still need to handle the practical aspects of the bully's behaviour.

The bully's intention is to exploit areas of vulnerability in your life. It is not to enable you to develop, grow and learn new skills so that you become a more effective person and employee. As such, you are entitled to defend yourself from these attacks even if you recognise that the bully has put their finger on a genuine area of weakness or lack of skill. Turning areas of vulnerability into areas of greater strength is in your best interests. Doing this will protect you. It will negate future bullying attacks in those areas of your life where you feel exposed, and will reduce the room for manoeuvre available to the bully.

This is the third step. You need to make up your own mind about what is true about you and what is not, and commit to learning the skills and behaviours which turn current areas of vulnerability into areas of strength. You can make a start at this task straightaway by identifying and committing to the facts and the truth about yourself, preparatory to rebuilding your self-confidence. Even if you have always been unassertive and struggled to feel confident, you can learn the skills of self-confidence. It is never too late to learn them. True self-confidence comes from knowing your strengths, learned skills and positive qualities, and using these characteristics as a basis for thinking well of yourself as a person and as an employee. You do not need to be accomplished at everything you do. But you do need to be competent at certain core skills and tasks. Knowing what your strengths are, and being really clear that you possess these strengths and can rely on your abilities in those areas, builds self-confidence. It means that when the bully attacks you with bogus criticisms about your performance, you can refute them absolutely then and there. There need be no debate. The conviction in your voice will preclude it. Of course, you need to be really honest with yourself as you formulate this list, and in it include areas in which you are skilled and competent rather than areas in which you are functional but not yet proficient, or areas in which you are below par and need to gain a greater breadth or depth of skills.

Start now by writing down all the skills and strengths you possess as an employee, and all the qualities you possess as a person. Write down any qualifications and awards you have earned. Write down all your achievements and all the positive outcomes you have created for yourself and others at work, and in your life. Commit all these things to paper. Take several days over this task, adding to the lists you generate as you identify more and more skills, strengths and positive attributes. Keep the lists somewhere in your home where you can see them so you can keep adding to them.

When they are complete, read the lists over and over until you have internalised these truths about yourself, and they become part of the way you think about yourself. Keep doing this until you can recite your strengths, skills and positive attributes without the prompt of the lists. Doing this will not make you arrogant. It will not result in you thinking you are better than other people. It will protect you. It will give you a realistic self-image based on the strengths, skills and qualities which you have developed.

Having compiled a thorough list of areas of strength and skill, and areas in which you need to develop, your next step is to buy yourself a notebook and pen which you like, and keep them by your bedside. Commit to writing in that notebook every night for at least the next four months before you turn the lights off. Each night, formulate three separate lists. Initially, you might start with only one or two items on each list. Over a period of a few days or weeks, your aim is to build up to a minimum of ten items per day for lists 1 and 2, and five items for list 3. Some of you who at a really low ebb might want to start with lists 1 and 2 only, and only introduce list 3 when you are ready.

The lists are as follows:

1. *Things you did well that day:* this list encompasses what you did well at work and outside of work. It might comprise simple facts such as you managed to dress yourself nicely for work that morning, that you got yourself into work even though you were shaking or crying beforehand, that you accomplished some of your work tasks effectively and spoke well at a certain meeting. It could also encompass some more challenging things that you did well at work that day such as handling a demanding situation well, making an effective rejoinder to a bullying remark, making it through the working day and getting home safely. You may also include items that are not work related such as the fact that you cooked a tasty meal that evening, managed to do the shopping on the way home, went to your class or hobby after work or sent a text to a friend to keep in touch.

2. *Things you are grateful for during that day:* this list comprises moments you enjoyed (perhaps the sunset or stroking your cat), resources that nourished you (perhaps a glass of wine or mug of herbal tea, or a consoling chat with a friend or family member), or other aspects of your life that supported you that day and added to your experience (perhaps having a home you like or good neighbours).

3. *Things that lightened your day:* this list comprises specific recollections of moments when you smiled or felt happy, however momentary that happiness might have been (perhaps your dog wagged their tail when you came home or you enjoyed smelling the roses in your garden) and specific actions that you took which

lightened your load that day (perhaps you treated yourself to your favourite food or drink or bought yourself a present on the way home).

When you have completed that day's list, re-read the list from the previous day. The benefit of making this commitment to yourself is that you go to sleep with good recollections and positive associations in your mind. You go to sleep thinking about *all the things you did well that day.* In and of itself, this counteracts the bullying criticisms you received that day. However, over a number of weeks and months, this exercise enables you to build your self-confidence and well-being as, just before you go to sleep, you persistently focus your mind on what you have done well, what you are grateful for and actions you took which contributed positively to your experience of that day. These thoughts nourish you during your sleep and enable your levels of self-confidence to rise.

What You Believe About Yourself Is Your Reality

One of the consequences of an effective campaign orchestrated by a team bully can be that you start to think less well of yourself:

- An effective campaign which targets your inner self could result in you generating thoughts that you are not a worthwhile or valuable person.

- An effective campaign which targets your performance could result in you generating thoughts that you are not competent to do your role and ought to be in a less responsible or well-paid job.

- An effective campaign which targets your reputation, contributing to a series of deteriorating relationships with colleagues, could result in you generating thoughts that no one in your team values your input or likes you.

In none of these cases are the evolving thoughts, or the beliefs which underpin them, truthful. They are more a reflection of the anguish you feel *but as long as the life-defeating, negative thoughts and beliefs remain unchallenged in your mind they will cause you continuing, unnecessary emotional distress.*

Your beliefs are unique to you. They are your personal principles and they guide your behaviour, thoughts and feelings. Your beliefs influence your values, inform your opinions and are often the basis on which you make your decisions. Your beliefs are mightily powerful tools. *They determine your experience of your reality*. You may have generated your core beliefs about life and yourself many years ago, and they may have been influenced by your family, faith, political and social traditions. You may not have consciously examined them before. But, now that you have been targeted by a team bully, it is important that you review your beliefs and consciously choose to replace unrealistic, unjust, harsh beliefs with more realistic, fair and compassionate ones, ones which inevitably provide you with life-enhancing, life-giving, trustworthy principles as the bedrock of your life.

It is vital that you replace life-defeating beliefs with life-affirming alternatives. Doing this will greatly reduce the room for manoeuvre that the bully has during any future attacks, enabling you to hear potentially destructive bullying remarks without being unduly influenced or upset by them. Why? Because it enables you to *listen to and believe in yourself* in the moment of an attack, reducing the impact of the bully's untruthful, unjust and critical words and actions.

The following exercise encourages you to identify any beliefs which you may hold which are not operating in your highest best interests and replace them with life-enhancing alternatives. It is a good idea to undertake this exercise in conjunction with the exercises on building self-confidence outlined above so that any self-limiting beliefs that operate in your life won't continue to undermine your self-confidence.

The first step is to write down what you think, feel and believe about yourself. Don't censor yourself as you do this. Simply take a piece of paper and start writing down what comes into your head as you focus on yourself. Some of what you write will be what you think about yourself, some will be what you feel, and some will be beliefs you hold about yourself. For the purposes of this exercise, these distinctions don't matter. What matters is that you capture your self-talk and write it down. Take as long as you need to do this, writing down anything that comes into your mind over several days. Then, once you have completed your list, start the process of challenging every one of the items on it to test the extent to which it is true. Just because something *feels* true, doesn't mean that it *is* true. For something to *be* true, there must be an objective, factual basis for it. Really challenge yourself. What objective, factual basis can you find to support each item on your list? If you can't find any supporting evidence, draw a line through it and, on a second sheet of paper, generate an alternative instead. Here are some examples:

Self-Defeating Feelings, Thoughts and Beliefs	Life-Giving Feelings, Thoughts and Beliefs
1. I am failing at my job.	1. I may FEEL as if I am failing at my job but the TRUTH is that I am competent at many aspects of my job and am well qualified to perform it, but I am experiencing a dip in self-confidence which means I don't always feel that way.
2. I am isolated and alone, and don't think I can carry on. No one in my team supports me or cares about the fact that I am being bullied.	2. I haven't much support at work right now but I can learn to protect myself from team bullying and then I won't need the team's support. I care that I am being bullied, and I do have access to books and sources of support outside work.
3. I am overwhelmed by the bullying and don't think I can change enough to handle it effectively.	3. I am daunted by the extent of the bullying but that won't stop me from learning what I need to learn so this never happens to me again.
4. I'm not assertive and don't want to become arrogant.	4. Right now, assertive behaviour is a challenge for me but I am determined to learn it and NOT to become arrogant as a result.

Let's now apply the principles we have been considering to the following examples:

- A secondary school teacher is subject to team bullying in her department by two of her peers. The attacks take place in the staff room in full hearing of the rest of the departmental team. None of her colleagues says anything to the secondary school teacher at the time of an attack or afterwards. As her self-confidence plummets, she begins to believe that she is in the wrong job. Confused by the critical feedback and obvious distaste for her opinions professed by the bullies, she starts to entertain thoughts that she isn't up to the task of managing a class of unruly teenagers, isn't robust or energetic enough for the busy inner-city school where she is employed, and isn't intelligent enough to hold her own in departmental meetings. There is no evidence to support any of these beliefs. The secondary school teacher draws much of her identity from her occupation as a teacher and, before the campaigns against her, drew much of her self-esteem from her work performance. Unable to distinguish between the truth about her and the bullying criticisms, she takes the bullying remarks to heart and quickly loses self-confidence and self-belief. It is only when she sits down one weekend with a long-standing friend that she starts to gain some perspective over her situation. She recognises that she has always been an effective teacher, that she has always enjoyed her job, and that she is giving too much weight to the bullying opinions of her two peers. She returns to work on Monday morning with renewed determination and resolve. Although the campaigns against her continue, both bullies experience her as more challenging to assault. She doesn't react to their attacks with either distress or vulnerability. Instead, she hardens her expression and cuts each bullying conversation short, saying she has a meeting to attend.

- An engineer in a manufacturing plant is subject to team bullying by his supervisor. Unused to receiving criticism about his work, he experiences a sudden dip in self-esteem and has trouble sleeping. The bullying remarks of his supervisor play on his mind and he becomes confused, partly because they are uttered in the hearing of his team colleagues, none of whom intervenes on his behalf. Initially, he thinks he might sit down with the bully and talk over the comments which have troubled him the most. But he recognises the folly of this idea, and quickly changes his mind. Instead, he commits to writing down every one of the bullying remarks which has upset him. Once on paper, the bullying remarks don't hold the same power over him. He considers each one and writes alongside it evidence which disproves it. Initially, this is a struggle for him. But as he perseveres, he finds it easier to refute the false allegations made against him. He uses a combination of his track record as an effective engineer, his previous positive performance reviews, and his belief that a good engineer doesn't become a poor engineer overnight. Some of his confidence returns immediately. He goes to work the following day, taking his notes with him to remind him of the truth about himself and his performance. The next time the bully attacks his performance, he lets him finish speaking and says: 'I don't believe that my performance is worthy of being characterised like that. Let's review the facts.'

- A librarian in a busy university library becomes subject to team bullying from an envious junior member of the team. The bully attacks the librarian's low-key demeanour and under-stated style, qualities which the brash and tactless bully secretly admires but feigns to pity. The campaign targets the librarian's inner self and personal qualities which the bully characterises as 'dull', 'tedious' and 'unimaginative'. Initially distressed by a series of personal attacks, the librarian is appalled that none of her colleagues stands up for her. She goes home that evening and cries. Then she gets out the box of cards, letters and treasures which her friends and relatives have given to her over the years, and starts to read them. She writes down all the compliments which she has received and commits them to memory. The next time the bully attacks her, in the silence of her mind she repeats the truth about her character to herself and when the bully finishes speaking she says: 'Is that all? I have to get on' and bends her head to her work.

In each of these examples, the campaigns against the targets are on-going. But in each case the target finds a way to mitigate the impact of the bullying attacks. They achieve this by *changing their relationship with the bullying remarks*, giving less weight to the words of the bullies and more weight to their own opinions and beliefs about their talents, characteristics, skills and competencies. As a consequence, each of them displays a greater level of resilience in the face of bullying and is less punctured by the on-going attacks. Their willingness to *confront their own beliefs, feelings and thoughts* is life-giving to each of them, even though they remain without support from their colleagues during the remainder of the campaigns against them.

Let's now turn our attention to an important issue which many of you may be contemplating: whether or not to make a formal complaint against the team colleague who bullied you.

Making a Formal Complaint

As part of your desire to regain lost ground and place responsibility where it rightly belongs, you may consider making a formal complaint about team bullying. Making a complaint is a very personal decision. On the surface, it is often motivated by a wish to call the bully to account and hold up their actions to scrutiny in the light of your employer's anti-bullying policy. This is a reasonable desire but is often not the whole story. Often the desire to see the complaint upheld can also be for quite different, personal and sometimes, hidden reasons. As there may be other outcomes from an investigation process that initially you might not be fully aware of, it is worth exploring your motives thoroughly before embarking on a formal complaint. Let's examine each of these desired outcomes in turn.

Justice

The desire for justice is entirely understandable but it is not necessarily straightforward to achieve. The issues may be clear cut and obvious to you. The bullying may have been witnessed by some of your team colleagues, some of whom may privately acknowledge to you the wrongdoing they have observed. But, even under those circumstances, it does not mean that you are guaranteed a just outcome. Getting full and complete evidence from team colleagues and other witnesses can be challenging, even in a formal investigation. Some of your colleagues may be afraid that they will be targeted if they testify against the bully. Others may be afraid of reprisals especially if the bully is their team manager or an influential member of staff. Even if some of your colleagues are prepared to provide full and complete evidence, a just outcome is still not assured because it can be hard to prove the *intention to bully*. In my experience, skilled team bullies can be highly adept at influencing the opinion of key people in the organisation at important junctures. They can put on a convincing display of ignorance, saying that they didn't know they were hurting you. They could say that they are appalled at the allegations against them, that they didn't intend to bully and that you are taking things the wrong way. They may even try to turn the tables on you by portraying you as a troublesome, ineffective or malingering member of staff. Equally problematic is that some HR investigators, whilst they want to arrive at a just outcome, may not have sufficient understanding about the complex dynamics at play in team bullying.

Closure

A second context for making a formal complaint could be your desire to bring closure to your experiences. You may hope that a just outcome to a formal complaint will enable you to walk away from a distressing chapter in your life. Bringing closure and having a formal complaint upheld are two separate things. Having a formal complaint upheld in and of itself will not necessarily enable you to move on. Instead, what can happen is that the judgement comes through one way or the other, and the trauma remains. Equally, if the judgement is against you, your levels of distress and anger at the injustice can increase as insult is added to injury.

Validation of Your Experiences

Receiving validation of your experiences is a central aspect of your healing from team bullying. This is because a core part of the experience of trauma is the aloneness and self-doubt that comes from being abused. In the silence of your heart you may be asking yourself: 'Did the bully really say those things to me? How could my colleagues sit silently and still, doing nothing, when the bully attacked me?'

Validation or witnessing by an empathic listener enables you to heal. The healing comes as a compassionate person hears what you have experienced and empathises with your distress. This quality of interaction enables you to digest the experience, process it and move on from it feeling more intact than before. Some of you will be able to receive the gift of validation from trusted friends and family members.

Others of you, particularly those who have been severely impacted by team bullying, may need to work with an experienced practitioner to achieve this closure.

Making a formal complaint doesn't mean that you will be heard or that your experiences will be validated. It means that someone, probably from HR, will initiate your organisation's formal complaints process and that *their role will involve handling that process impartially.* Their job is not to listen to you in the empathic way you may need. It is to manage the process of the complaint. A skilled HR practitioner may well prove to be an insightful and empathic listener, and you may benefit greatly from talking with them. But, equally, you may find that the HR investigator assigned to your case doesn't have superior listening skills or is only an averagely empathic person. In this case, you may be disappointed by the quality of your interactions with them, even though they are handling their role as investigator quite competently.

To Prevent the Bully from Targeting a Team Colleague

A fourth reason to make a formal complaint is to draw attention to what has happened to you in the hope of preventing a team colleague from being targeted in the future. This altruistic reason is very well-intentioned and often comes from a desire to take steps which preclude other people from suffering in the way you have. However, the only person who can prevent the bully from bullying in the future is the bully themselves. A complaints process can't compel them to amend their ways, although one of the recommendations arising from a successful complaint could be that the bully is required to participate in coaching or training aimed at addressing their bullying behaviour.

Your primary responsibility is to yourself as you learn to combat team bullying effectively so *you* are not subject to a successful campaign in the future. You do not have to carry the burden of preventing your colleagues from being targeted. They can do that work for themselves.

Making a Complaint

Overall, if you have weighed up the pros and cons associated with making a formal complaint and have decided to proceed, be prepared for a potentially time-consuming and onerous process. There will be work to do documenting your case, attending meetings, and discussing the evidence, all of which will require your time and energy when your internal resources are already thinly stretched coping with the impact of the campaign against you.

I cannot tell you whether or not to make a complaint, as that decision is very personal to you, but I do advise that you go into it only after careful thought and preparation, knowing what is involved, and with your eyes wide open. However, you do not have to rely on a favourable outcome to an investigation in order to move on with your life. You can do this for yourself by doing the work of recovery and, as a separate issue, make a formal complaint if you want to.

Bringing Closure

So how do you bring closure to experiences of team bullying? The simple answer is: you decide to. You make the decision to move on and bring closure to your experiences once you have processed your trauma, replaced self-defeating thoughts and beliefs with life-giving alternatives, and learned sufficient self-protective skills that you no longer feel vulnerable to future attack. At that point, you can start to look forward again and make plans which may or may not include seeking employment elsewhere.

If you decide to stay in your current organisation, do so as a positive decision, one that is right for you given the issues involved in moving employer and starting again somewhere else. If you decide to leave your current organisation, again do so as a positive decision, one which will enable you to work in a healthier team dynamic and rediscover your enthusiasm and energy for being part of an effective team.

Summary of Key Points from the Chapter

Being subject to team bullying involves you in handling dual challenges. You face challenges that originate in the world outside yourself as the bully attacks you, undermines your credibility and injures your team relationships. You face challenges that originate in the world inside yourself as your self-confidence tumbles, you start to generate critical thoughts and beliefs about yourself, and your self-doubt and anxiety levels escalate. Recovery from experiences of team bullying involves processing trauma to heal your emotions; replacing self-critical thoughts and life-defeating beliefs with life-enhancing, truthful alternatives; and learning self-protective strategies to combat bullying attacks.

Waiting to be rescued is understandable when you are beleaguered and under attack. But don't get stuck waiting for rescue – it is a futile thing to do. Instead, commit to *rescuing yourself* by setting up life-enhancing dynamics in your life which preclude a would-be bully from grooming you, and enable you to confront a team bully simply and straightforwardly.

Your aim is to live out of the fullest expression of your personal power, using assertive and confident behaviour as a matter of course in your day-to-day working life. Living out of the fullest expression of your personal power means taking responsibility for the thoughts, feelings and beliefs you generate about yourself, choosing to remain composed when under attack, and demonstrating to the bully that you retain full authority over your life and well-being.

It is vital that you find ways to process your trauma so that you can free yourself from the potentially debilitating symptoms of unprocessed trauma. You need to make a firm commitment to yourself to challenge your mental self by rooting out any untrue or negative self-talk and replacing it with life-giving, factual self-talk. Confidence is a learned skill and, like any skill, can be learned at any stage of your life. True confidence comes from knowing your strengths, skills and positive attributes. Knowing what these are gives you the ability to listen to yourself, rather than the bully, during an attack designed to undermine you.

Your beliefs are the principles upon which you build your life. They are mightily powerful tools. Your beliefs determine your experience of your reality. It is vital that you commit to living according to beliefs which are life-enhancing and which protect you against bullying. Very little that a bully says to you during an attack is likely to be true. Don't listen to their bullying words. Listen to your own beliefs about your value and your competence instead. Should a bully target your fears about yourself, your areas of self-doubt or an area of under-developed skill, you are still entitled to defend yourself against the attack.

Making a formal complaint for team bullying is a personal decision. An investigation can involve an onerous and time-consuming process, and may not go the way you want even if the issues are crystal clear from your point of view. If you want to make a complaint, be clear what any personal, potentially hidden outcomes you may be looking for (justice, closure, validation or to prevent an attack on someone else) and go into the process with your eyes open.

When the time is right for you, you will be able to bring closure to your experiences of team bullying. To arrive at this point you need to process any trauma you may be carrying, replace life-defeating thoughts and beliefs with life-giving alternatives, and learn to protect yourself at the time of any future attack. You may or may not decide to move to a different employer, but you will be ready to move on and close a painful chapter of your life having acquired greater self-confidence, greater resilience and greater self-belief than you had before you were bullied in your team.

To everyone who has read this far, I hope that reading this book has been a rewarding experience for you. I trust that it has enabled you to acquire valuable strategies, insights and know-how so that you can recover from your experiences of team bullying, become bully-proof and move on with greater wisdom, self-belief and resilience. I send you my best wishes for your recovery and future life.

Lightning Source UK Ltd.
Milton Keynes UK
UKHW01f0614210818
327557UK00010B/397/P